Pushy

By
Jo Mangum

Published by:
Intermedia Publishing, Inc.
P.O. Box 2825
Peoria, Arizona 85380
www.intermediapub.com

ISBN 978-1-935906-97-1

To my students who ended up teaching me.

To my friends for all of their encouragement.

To my writing coaching, Linda Rohrbough, who helped me take an idea and turn it into something more.

To my husband, Tom, who has stayed true to his vow and allowed me to pursue my dreams even when it meant sacrifice… I am deeply grateful.

Contents

Chapter 1
Asking "The" Question — 1

Chapter 2
The Beast Within Us All — 13

Chapter 3
Are You Listening? — 21

Chapter 4
Breaking Up Is Hard To Do — 33

Chapter 5
I Want To Go That Way! — 47

Chapter 6
What Would You Do If You Could Not Fail? — 61

Chapter 7
The 30-Day Plan; Putting It Into Action — 77

Chapter 8
Beliefs vs. Doubt··· And The Winner Is··· — 93

Chapter 9
May I Have This Dance? — 107

Chapter 10
Who Is Your Eleanor? — 121

Chapter 11
Send, Call, See, Post — 137

Chapter 12
Actions Require Asking — 157

Chapter 13
The Belay — 179

Chapter 14
Pushy – Finding Your Process — 199

Chapter 1
Asking "The" Question

It's my normal teaching day. The topic is how to explode your profits by cultivating referrals from your sphere of influence. As I survey the group of salespeople in front of me, they seem to have little in common... there's a variety of ages, cultures, and education levels. But I know shortly they will unite together with a collective problem, and that problem will become my problem.

It starts with one person raising their hand and asking what I call "THE question." I call it this because there is a 100 percent chance that it's going to be asked. It always is. Once asked, the rest of the students will nod their heads in agreement and mutter praise to the person for having the courage to ask it. Then they'll all turn and look at me, with faces of anxious defiance, waiting for the answer.

What does everyone want to know?

Why is it so important?

And why is this topic so emotional that the group collectively had a visceral response?

Let me answer the second question first. I tell my sales classes the most important thing they need for success and a strong long-term business is a steady flow of referrals. This is number one. No referrals means a salesperson has to work twice as hard with less pay. In fact, no referrals means there is real danger of the business failing. So when I emphasize the importance of referrals, I get no arguments from the class. They all voice acknowledgement and agreement. But...

As for why "THE question" I get asked most is so emotional, the answer is... because it threatens loss. Loss of relationships the salesperson values the most, loss of the current roles they play in people's lives, loss of themselves by becoming the type of salesperson they hate. This sense of loss is so strong that it overwhelms the desire for gain. So many people simply ignore it. So what is the question everyone wants to know the answer to?

How do I ask for referrals without appearing pushy to my friends and family?

The funny thing is, I was the one in my class who asked "THE question" when training for my real estate business. At the time I started, my background was in project management. The uncomfortable switch to being an entrepreneur that sells, or what I call a "salespreneur," was a product of my desire to change my life. I was sick of my job.

I had started my career in corporate America a decade ago and threw myself into building my vision of success. Working for a small software development company, I thrived on the long hours and the crazy travel schedule. My idea of happiness was "five cities in five days." Because of hard work from me and many other like-minded people, the company had amazing success. In fact, it had enough success that a large corporation moved in and purchased it. This provided wealth for the owners and a radical lifestyle change for the employees.

The employees went from being an integral part of the day-to-day decisions to being ignored. We went from flexibility in our schedules (because we worked long hours) to a strict time schedule. We went from an interpretive dress code to charts that listed the preferred color of panty hose, the length of our skirts, and the height of our heels. But more importantly, we suddenly had no control over our destiny... no matter how you performed you received the same annual increase as the person who did the minimum required to get by. I was suffocating.

I wanted more. Hard work was not an obstacle but I wanted to be paid for that hard work. AND I wanted the freedom to control my schedule. So I became an entrepreneur that sells or what I call a salespreneur. Before I go any further, does this in any way sound familiar to you?

Although enthusiastic and energetic, I had no real sales skill. To say my learning curve was sharp would be an understatement. In a rigorous training program, I learned all the basic skills, like overcoming objections and conversational prospecting. I was also educated on the most productive form of prospecting, which is cultivating your sphere of influence (SOI). This is when things got scary for me.

As a native of the city where I worked, my SOI was deep. There were literally hundreds of people who knew me, or at least knew of me, hopefully in a favorable light. However, when I started my business, I completely ignored my SOI. I did this even though I understood and acknowledged their benefit to my business. When questioned by my business coach about why I ignored my SOI, I said work with strangers was easier because they don't know I'm new!

Two years later I was exhausted from the hours it took to chase and close cold leads. I had to acknowledge that I had a problem. Actually make that plural… I had problems. I was afraid to work with my SOI and as a result nobody in my "sphere" even knew about my career. My best friends and family barely knew where I went during the day. When I started to take a hard look at this, I uncovered barriers I'd constructed in my mind about working with my SOI.

First, many of my SOI had known me for decades, which meant they experienced first- hand some bad periods in my life's history. (For example, I loved bad men and good gin in my 20s.) How could I now hold myself up as someone to be trusted with their biggest investment?

Worse, asking my SOI for "help" felt so bad. Every time I considered uttering the phrase all the sales gurus recommended, I felt sick. I couldn't make myself say, "I need your help… if you know of someone who needs help buying or selling a home, would you let me know?" I realized my sick feeling was due to a vision that popped into my head of me as Oliver Twist, the poor orphaned boy asking for more porridge.

But most important, I was convinced even if I could make myself "man up" and ask my SOI to use my services or refer me, I would lose all of my relationships. In my mind friends and family would abandon all communication and affiliation as soon as I uttered those words.

Knowing I needed to ask for referrals I would frequently make a list of everyone I was going to call in a particular day and then find excuses why I shouldn't call. So at the end of the day I had once again broken a promise to myself. Day after day of this broken promise pounded my confidence.

But then I meet a fellow salesperson, Margie. Margie, who worked exclusively with her SOI, had a business where she worked thirty-hour weeks and made well over six-figures each year. But most impressive was that her large SOI, the very ones that used her services and referred people to her, loved her, wanted her to be successful, and actively looked for potential prospects for her business! Drawn to her, I decided to model my business after her business. But what specifically did she do? Working up courage I approached Margie about being my mentor. The sun was shining on me that day because she agreed. Working under Margie I learned many things... how often she communicated with them, how she communicated her value, and how she asked them for referrals. All of this information was incredible and essential to converting my business model. But it was not the source of power for Margie's business. The secret was in her beliefs.

You see, all of Margie's behavior—how she talked to people, what she said—the tone in her voice—all her actions reflected her beliefs. These beliefs were simple; I am important in people's lives. I use my skills to protect them and help them make good decisions. In short, they need me and I am best for them.

Once I had met Margie and understood the power of her belief system, I became increasingly aware of other salespeople with the same beliefs.

Gary is a financial planner who is very successful helping people place their money in profitable areas. His business is completely referral based because he works hard at teaching satisfied clients to be his advocate. Gary reports that he says to clients (in person and via correspondence), "I need your help. My business is built on satisfied clients telling others about my services. Could you be my eyes and ears out in the community and let me know when you see anyone who needs a competent financial planner?" When I heard his pitch I felt a sense of nausea come over me at the thought of saying those words. Inquiring about what he felt when he asked, he replied, "There are lots of bad planners out there and I need to make sure that they tell people about mine because I care about people and their results." Again, it was about his belief system backed up by skills.

Laura was a real estate agent (Remember that real estate is the industry I sold in so I have lots of real estate agent examples. But there is a strong common denominator in this industry and many others in that it's a serviced-based industry. Many do not realize but most agents are in the business of selling their services, not houses.) who approached me about helping her with a potential new listing because she was uncomfortable with the area and I was an expert in the area. The house, the situation, and the people were awful. When we got back in the car I was forming the words "Run from this listing Laura!" when I heard her say, "Wow, they really need me. There's no way they can sell that house without me!" Wow was right… they did need her. But more astoundingly, she was committed to helping them. Where I would have turned the listing down, she sold that house, helped them buy a new house, and has received multiple referrals from them.

As evidence mounted that the successful salespeople had a core belief about their worth to the client I looked deep to understand what I believed. What a difference! I believed that my SOI would see me as pushy. I believed they would see me as needy (something along the lines of "Poor Jo, she can't get a job so now she's a salesperson"). I believed there were many more salespeople just like me that could help them and do a fine job at it so why pick me.

I realized my beliefs were killing my business.

Now I had a new problem. How would I change my entire group of beliefs? The process was a substantial one. But I did it. Gradually, using several techniques, my mindset began to change. I surprised myself one day when I realized I looked forward to talking with my SOI about my business. I sought out ways to bring value to their lives. Nothing gave me greater pleasure.

Sounds good, right? But how did it translate into performance? Well, my first year with this new set of beliefs resulted in a six-fold increase in my bottom line. Yes… really. And you can have a substantial increase in your business too.

I know this because it wasn't long before fellow sales associates began noticing the acceleration in my business and there were lots of knocks at my office door. I believe what goes around comes around, so I started teaching these principles. Now, years later, I've worked with thousands of salespeople.

And this experience taught me many things….

The most important thing I learned is this: the fear of appearing pushy is the #1 barrier most salespeople have when reaching out to their SOI. I have heard every excuse in the world (and made every excuse in the world myself) but the bottom line is still the bottom line. Your SOI has to understand that your business lives on referrals and you have to be skilled in asking for those referrals. To be successful at this (and by successful I mean you love doing it and it works) you must have two things: a strong skillset and a strong mindset.

Skillset

Skillset is the collection of sales skills you need to effectively perform in your profession. To be effective at cultivating your SOI requires several skills… create and maintain a "drip" system, convert a casual conversation into an opportunity for referrals, acknowledging and answering objections, working with various personality types, and working through the emotions of their clients. These are critical skills that every salesperson needs. Roughly half of this book addresses these skills by providing a simple how-to model for creating a sphere of influence system that I've taught to thousands of students. This system shows not only how to organize your SOI but how often to contact them, what to say, and most importantly how to add significant value to their lives.

It may sound time consuming (which it is). It may sound difficult (which it's not). But the good news is these skills are learnable. Yes, it takes practice. Yes, it takes commitment. Yes, it takes hard work. All it takes to succeed is "want to." This brings me to mindset, or the set of beliefs.

Mindset

Mindset is more complicated because we have a lifetime of experiences that led to the creation of beliefs. Once we have developed these beliefs they are very controlling and very resistant to change. Identifying the limiting beliefs and changing them is at the center of learning how to manage your mind. Managing your mind includes understanding your motivation, identifying and changing beliefs, stopping negative self-talk, and handling negative emotion. The first part of this book is how to work on your mindset.

Where are we going?

The book is divided into three sections: one on training you mind, the second on building a skillset for cultivating your sphere of influence, and lastly a section where both the mind and skill section converge.

I have intentionally made most of the chapters small knowing that most salespreneurs struggle with time. This was no easy task because I could talk (and write) for hours on this subject. BUT the point of this book is to synthesize all that I have learned and give it to you in an easy format. All that being said, there is one word of warning....

A Word of Warning

Being a salespreneur I know you are a doer. You look at this information and think, "Okay, I'll just skip to the 'how' section, implement it, and get back to business." Certainly, you can do that. You will learn something that can be applied immediately. BUT you will be leaving behind the important information: management of your mind. Although mind management is the harder work, you will be creating skills that will last you the rest of your life.

Now that you know what's ahead to help make you successful, I want to end this chapter with one more tool for you. At the end of each chapter, I'll provide you with "Five Things to Remember From This Chapter." This will help you hang on to the most important concepts I've gained from my experience training successful salespreneurs. Next I'll show you how to start taming that beast in your head.

Five Things to Remember From this Chapter

1. Every salespreneur worries about being pushy, especially with their SOI.

2. You can ask for referrals, receive referrals, and everyone continue to love you. Really.

3. There are two ingredients to successfully get referrals and still maintain your relationships: "Skillset" and "Mindset."

4. "Skillset" is learnable.

5. "Mindset" requires that you learn how your mind works and how to manage it.

Mindset

Chapter 2

The Beast Within Us All

Ah… Monday morning; new beginning for the salespreneur. This is the day to forget the disappointments of last week and start fresh with new goals. And so was the case for Jack.

The previous year he had been down-sized from a corporate position. Determined to be his boss, Jack surveyed his skills and decided to open a handy-man service. He had always loved that type of work and felt that he could marry this work to his corporate experience and create a profitable business. But it was a hard decision. Mostly because so many of his friends and family voiced concerns. They felt like he was wasting his education and experience. Although he understood their concerns (he was concerned about it also), he moved forward because he liked the idea of working with his hands but most importantly working for himself.

Jack created a business plan that reflected a referral-based strategy. To support that strategy Jack had compiled a data base of his SOI and created a monthly newsletter to communicate with them. Although Jack had received referrals, he needed more. After evaluating the plan, he added phone calls to his SOI as a business strategy. During these calls he planned on creating awareness of his new business and asking them to pass the word along to their SOI about his services.

Armed with a list of people to call, Jack had scheduled himself to call five people a day for each week day. When he ran out of names then he'd start over again. Today was the day to start the new strategy.

Fast forward to Friday… the good news was Jack had a busy week. There were several jobs he'd completed and many other supportive activities like working on his website. The bad news was Jack had not called any of the people slated for this week. Oh well, Jack thought, I can start again on Monday.

Ah… another Monday to start fresh and another Friday for Jack to realize he had not completed (or even started his calls).

This is a very familiar tale for most salespreneurs. We identify goals, strategies, and actions. We have the skills and enthusiasm to execute and yet we don't. We are smart. We are motivated. We know how. We know why. And yet we don't. What's up with that?

What's up is our amazing and powerful brain. Let me explain.

How Our Brain Works

Our brain has three parts. The Thinker, the Believer, and the Regulator.

The Thinker

The Thinker is the part of your brain that thinks, perceives, and makes decisions. Jack used his Thinker to create his business plan, decide on strategies, and write his weekly activities list.

But our Thinker needs help with this work. It needs all of our past experiences to inform decisions. Think about it, the older we get the more experiences we have. The more experiences we have the better our decisions become. Enter the Believer.

The Believer

The Believer is this massive computer in our brain that stores everything that has happened to us in our lifetimes. Many of these experiences created beliefs and they are stored here. The Believer knows what we like and don't like, how we feel about things and people, what we avoid and what we embrace, what we are ashamed of (everybody has something), how we see ourselves, etc. The rub here is that not all of the beliefs that are stored are true. They were formed by incorrect information (we will talk more about this later). The point here is our Believer is the advisor of the Thinker... where important decisions are made.

The Regulator

This part of your brain has a fairly simple yet very powerful job. It resolves the conflicts between the Thinker and the Believer (we will see an example of this in Jack). Yes, they often have conflicts and the Regulator wants to keep peace in the brain so it decides which one is correct and quietly fixes the problem. I say quietly because the Regulator has an entire arsenal at its disposal and often deploys methods that our Thinkers can't perceive.

Let's apply this information to Jack.

Jack used his Thinker to make the decision to start a handyman business, create a plan, and begin the execution of the plan. He had read many books on creating a referral-based business and knew that the addition of a calling component was a logical step to create more business. All great decisions.

Jack Believer also assisted him in creating this plan by reminding his Thinker about a similar business model he had seen work well. But… Jack's Believer also remembered the nay-sayers about his business, many were the very people on his call list. Because he believed that they were not supportive of his business he was concerned about talking with them. And the truth be known, he had that nagging thought that maybe calling really wasn't such a good idea.

Jack had a conflict between his Thinker (his business plan) and his Believer mind (people aren't supportive of me and my business). Enter the Regulator.

The Regulator looks at the situation and decides which one wins… the business plan or the memory of the nay-sayers. How does it decide? Whichever one is strongest.

In Jack's case the Regulator determined that the memory and the feelings related with the nay-sayers was stronger than his vision of the business plan. The result was the Regulator helped Jack "forget" to make calls. He chose other activities (working on his website, etc.) instead. Were these activities important? Certainly. More important than the calls? Probably not.

When confronted with the choices he made, Jack defended them strongly saying he had been so busy he just didn't have the time. See the power of the Regulator… it convinced him that not executing his carefully considered business plan was okay.

Bottom line: Our behavior follows our beliefs

This is a great brain system that stops us from being in a state of insanity. A great system unless, of course, our beliefs are incorrect. In fact, Jack had formed a belief that people were judging him based on one person's comments. He had ignored the people that had been supportive. So now his decisions are being controlled by a flawed belief. Why do we accept one person's negative opinion over the support of many others? Great question. I'll tell you in a minute!

Here's another example.

I was brought up the youngest of four children, so there is natural sibling competition. My oldest sister had a high IQ and she performed really well in school. My intelligence level could best be described as average. When report cards came, the differences in our IQs were obvious. To ensure that I was not completely crushed my mother would say, "Yes, you are average and average is good." So a belief formed in me that I am an average person.

As my sales career took off (thanks to learning how to work my SOI), I enjoyed several production milestones. However, when my picture was displayed in the office as a sales leader for the month, I became livid and demanded that it be taken down. I knew my behavior wasn't rational nor was it typical behavior (I'm not prone to fits of rage) but I simply could not help myself. As I began to learn more about how underlying beliefs can dictate behavior I uncovered this—my picture being displayed as a sign of success meant I was above average, not average. That created a conflict between my Thinker and my Believer. My Thinker was performing at a higher level than my Believer thought I should. My Regulator stepped in demanding my picture be taken down, and that solved the problem. Demanding my picture be taken down didn't make me stop to take a look at my beliefs at that point, because I was still producing. But this next part did.

I noticed after experiencing these successes for a while, I continued to set higher production goals. Then as I got close to the new goal, I would stop prospecting. In other words, my Regulator stepped in and made sure that the belief of "I'm average" stayed true.

I was a classic example. I had a deeply held belief (I'm average) that when evidence was presented to the contrary (production leader) it would cause an outburst of anger. And when I attempted to push past this belief to achieve even higher levels of production, I told myself all the reasons why success was a bad idea. I remember saying things to myself like it would mean more work hours or I would have to hire an assistant I couldn't afford.

By the way, I am anything but average. I know that now. I didn't know that then. But half of my sales career was controlled by that belief. Bummer.

Let's think about this. We all have a set of beliefs, some true some not. Regardless of their accuracy, our behavior is established using them.

To demonstrate this point, let's use the analogy of driving. I get into my car with the intention of going to the grocery store. I buckle my seat belt, start the car, and put it into drive. Then I look in my rear view mirror, and using only what I can see in the rear mirror, I attempt to drive forward to the store. Yikes! That's essentially how our brains work.

So, what beliefs are limiting your effectiveness? Here are just a few I frequently hear:

- I'm not sure why my services are better than anyone else?
- I've had a past experience with a pushy salesperson and I didn't like it.
- When I ask for help from someone I feel weak.

Do any of these sound familiar? They do for most of us.

The Good News

Regardless of whom you are, where you are from, or what you want, you have the power to receive it. We all consciously know this and have tried many times only to be disappointed. The key to changing the outcome is in the workings of our minds.

At the center of these workings is our belief system. Because all behavior follows our beliefs, changing our behavior means changing our beliefs. No easy task. But I have a plan. This plan is to learn how we get our beliefs and root out those beliefs that limit us. Then we are going to create a vision to give us the motivation to move through the steps. Lastly, we are going on a thirty-day plan. Sound like fun?

Five Things to Remember From this Chapter

1. Our mind has three parts: Thinker, Believer, and the Regulator.

2. The Thinker gets most of the information needed to make decisions from Believer.

3. The Believer gets its information from a variety of sources. Some of these sources are reliable, some are not.

4. The Regulator makes sure there is harmony between Thinker and the Believer.

5. Because of this system, the key to change is our belief system.

Chapter 3

Are You Listening?

My friend, Annette, is a tall, slim, statuesque, redhead. I am not. Spending time with her is wonderful except when we go shopping. In addition to having all these wonderful physical characteristics Annette is very wealthy (yes, beautiful and rich... sometimes life is not fair), which means she goes into shops where an evening bag costs $2000. I go into the shop with her but find myself very uncomfortable. When saying uncomfortable, I mean there is this visceral reaction. My brain is shouting loudly "Get me out of here!" Within five minutes of arrival to the shop I am on a bench outside of the shop waiting for her. When she asks me why I left the store I lie and say a phone call came in. Have you ever had a similar experience?

Is this reaction because I think the prices are crazy and want nothing to do with the merchandise? That's true but this kind of reaction means one thing... I believed I didn't belong there. Why? Who knows!

We all have a huge set of beliefs that controls how we see the world... all of it. Beliefs are a fundamental component in our lives. How we dress, who we have relationships with, where we shop, how we run our business—everything is affected by our belief system. These beliefs have been formed by experiences, by our culture, by our family, and by people that we consider authority figures. Then we perpetuate these beliefs by saying them over and over again to ourselves. To understand better, we are going to look at authority experiences and self-talk.

Authority Experiences

In the beginning of my selling career, I was eager to prospect, find customers, and make money. My eagerness led me to try a variety of prospecting methods. One day I put together a mailer to go to a group of potential prospects and was very excited about the anticipated outcome. In my enthusiasm, I told any one of my colleagues who would listen about this great mailer. A more experienced salesperson, who I considered successful, turned to me and said, "You know, honey, this idea has been tried many times and just doesn't work. Don't waste your money."

With terrible disappointment, I went back to my cubicle, threw the mailer in the trash, and never tried that prospecting method again. Why? Because this other salesperson, who I viewed as an authority figure, told me it didn't work, and a new belief was formed. I perpetuated this belief many times over the years by telling other new salespeople that the same prospecting method did not work. Not until years later, when I was presented with evidence to the contrary, did I change my belief.

I can name a dozen more instances in my life where someone in authority told me something and it became my belief. Just the simple power of suggestion and presto it's my belief too. Ironically, many of them (like I don't belong in high priced stores) are a product of childhood but continue to play themselves out in our adult lives. Of course in our childhood virtually anyone could be an authority figure… my friends' nine-year-old brother could have been an authority to my seven-year-old self. Unfortunately, he may have helped me form a belief that I still hold today and more importantly impacts my behavior today.

I feel certain that you are searching your memory banks right now for those situations or events when a belief was formed. Did someone say you weren't good at something? Your brain remembers. Did a teacher make a derogatory comment about you? Your brain remembers that too.

I can remember like it was yesterday. I was wearing a plaid skirt and my Mary Jane shoes. My third grade teacher, Miss Martin, smelled like ivory soap. Miss Martin asked me to hand her the eraser. Instead I handed her the chalk. Her response was to call me stupid in front of the class. That one incident has dictated many actions of my life. You might be saying, "Okay, that wasn't very nice, but it was a long time ago... get over it." You would be right. It's not that I'm not over it; it's that a belief developed from that moment and it's a belief that has impacted my life. I've often wondered if that's the reason I'm so compelled to get every certification, take every course, get educational degrees. Virtually everyone I know has had some experience from their childhood that has impacted them... I'm betting that you have a similar moment (or two or three) in your life. We all do.

The point is these experiences create who we are, what we believe, and how we behave.

Certainly all of these experiences have an impact on our behavior. But the biggest impact comes not from what another person told us but from what we tell ourselves.

Self-Talk

Fifty thousand. That's the estimate of how many times a day we talk to ourselves. That's a little over one per second. Basically our brains are running a continual mental commentary. You may not even be aware of it. It's like white noise that we don't consciously hear. But that doesn't make it any less lethal. Lethal? Yes, whatever is said in our self-talk guides our behavior, which makes it lethal.

Your Internal Conversation

Fortunately, Pam had a very big SOI. The number of people she knew was a significant factor in choosing to start a new business. She had enthusiastically mailed announcements to her SOI and had a great e-mail system that "dripped" on them monthly. So she kept herself "top of mind" with this important group. Her plan was brilliant, except for one thing. To get significant results from marketing to her SOI required that she call them. And she hated calling. But she decided to start making phone calls anyway.

The next day Pam made a list of people she would call. First up was Nancy, a long-time friend. Sitting in front of the phone, she took a moment to think about the call prior to dialing. That's when the trouble started. Her internal conversation sounded something like this...

I haven't talked to Nancy in a long time. Calling her now to remind her about my business doesn't feel quite right but I just need to do it. I wonder if she even knows that I changed professions. I wonder what she thought?

In Pam's self-talk she created feelings of being a little embarrassed. Those are the feelings she has just before she dials the phone.

After talking with Nancy, here's Pam's self-talk.

Hmmm… she seemed a little reserved. Just as I suspected she doesn't think I'm suited for this profession. Now I'm going to be embarrassed if I run into her again since I know how she feels. Well, she never really liked me. I think I'll just take her off my SOI list… it's probably better.

Wow… what a big leap to a conclusion! Seem ridiculous? It's not. This type of conversation happens frequently in the minds of salespeople. I literally have heard thousands talk about similar conversations.

Notice in that sample conversation, a couple of things happened. First, Pam began with feelings of being disingenuous (I'm calling someone I haven't talk to in a really long time for a self-serving reason.) and worried about what Nancy thought of her. After the conversation Pam jumped to a conclusion about what Nancy was thinking without any evidence. Nancy could have thought that it was so nice to talk to Pam. That didn't matter, Pam felt the response was negative and acted on her conclusion with removal of Nancy's name from the SOI list. She continues by having concerns about running into Nancy later at social occasions like the next community board meeting.

The whole situation left Pam feeling beaten down. No wonder she hates to make calls.

It's Not Just the Words

The words Pam said to herself were influential over her actions but they could not have affected her alone. For her self-talk to have this impact requires a picture and an emotion.

Words ⟹ *Pictures* ⟹ *Emotions*

Using the example of Pam:

Words: I don't think she likes me.

Picture: Visualizing bumping into her at a board meeting with a poor outcome.

Emotions: Feel beaten down.

Words, pictures, and emotions are the power combo for making self-talk into beliefs.

This is why some self-talk just passes through our brains without a second thought, but some self-talk sticks. Think about it… your most prominent memories and beliefs have emotions associated with them. Can you precisely recall a customer that complained? Absolutely. We may have constant chatter going through our brains, but the events that caused us to visualize and experience emotion are the ones that stick. Negative emotions are strong and often dominate our thoughts.

Types of Self-Talk

There are many types of self-talk. Let's look at each type.

Think things through—This is a review and interpretation of things happening in our lives. For example, as you are creating an e-mail to send to your SOI, you talk through the process with yourself. You might have an internal conversation going on about which subject line would get more attention or about the number of people on the list.

Past, Present, and Future Events—How They Help Us Interpret The Present.

Past—Many times we re-live events from the past. These events help us make decisions about how to handle current situations. In Pam's past, maybe she had a comfortable situation with Nancy before and those events guided how she reacted to the phone conversation. Another interaction with Nancy assisted Pam in deepening her beliefs.

Present—Many times we are talking to ourselves about current events in our life. We consider how it will affect us. This chatter can take a perfectly innocent conversation with a co-worker and turn it into something crazy. For example, a friend is a salesperson for a large pharmaceutical company that recently changed their CEO. The new CEO has made it very clear that there are changes coming. My friend has interpreted the CEO's intentions to mean she will be getting laid off. Is that true? Not necessarily... particularly because she is one of the highest producing salespeople. But fear clouds her interpretation of this present event.

Future—We project our beliefs on the future. I was recently out with a group of friends and the subject of the lottery came up and the huge sum of the current jackpot. When we compared notes, we realized that every single one of us began a conversation with ourselves about how we would spend the money.

Interpret interactions with others—Most of us frequently have interchanges with other people via work or home. After these interchanges, we continue to talk to ourselves. I frequently talk to myself about those things I wish my brain had come up with during the conversation. Sometimes I give meaning to conversations. For example, if I have a conversation with a client and they sounded guarded, I may find myself talking about what that meant and applying meaning. Like Pam, I might make up there's a problem in the relationship that doesn't exist.

Respond to experiences—Due to the nature of my sales business, there are frequent opportunities to solve problems. After a tense conversation, I re-hash the situation in my mind many times. Each time I'm just a little more brilliant in my responses! The more emotional the experience, the more we relive it in our inner conversations.

By the way, these internal conversations happen in a variety of ways… daydreaming, talking out loud (my husband's personal favorite), journaling, and making gestures.

Some of your self-talk is simply chatter that assists us in everyday decisions. Other self-talk elicits emotions both positive and negative. All self-talk drives behavior.

Let's look again at the scene between Pam and Nancy and their phone call. What would have happened if Pam's self-talk was positive before making the call?

Positive Self-talk

Although words, pictures, and emotions can create negative beliefs we can use that same power to reverse it into something positive.

Prior to calling Nancy, Pam could have this conversation with herself. *I think that my services would be a huge benefit to Nancy. I'll give her a call to make sure she received my announcement and see if she would like to get my newsletter.*

Do you think that Pam's conversation with Nancy would have been different if she started with this self-talk prior to the call? Of course. For one thing, the tone of Pam's voice would have been uplifting. Nancy might sense that positive energy and would have reacted with more enthusiasm. **Never underestimate that other people can hear and read the energy created by your self-talk.**

After a positive call Pam's inner dialog after the call may be: Wow, reconnecting with Nancy was great. She did seem a little distracted but we all are sometimes. I'll send her a note and make a follow-up call to her next month.

Notice this is a completely different experience than the first example. The differences can be attributed to Pam's beliefs about the value of her business. In addition to being a very different emotional experience for Pam, it had a different outcome. Instead of Pam dropping Nancy from her SOI list, she made the decision to drip on Nancy and scheduled another call.

You can change your experience, too. The key to moving your experiences with your SOI from the first example (where Pam doubted her value) to the second example (where Pam was proud of her services) is two critical things that must be present together.

Intercepting Your Self-Talk

PLUS

Changing Your Beliefs

What Is <u>Your</u> Negative Self-Talk?

Are you a good listener? Most of us are not. There is so much noise in our lives that we miss quite a lot. That also goes for our self-talk. It's been such a constant sound for so long we just tune it out. In fact, this internal conversation can be so tuned out that many don't believe they have self-talk. But I can prove it.

Do this exercise… take off all of your clothes, stand in front of a mirror, and listen. Shhh… listen carefully, it's there! Yes, I proved my point, so let's do a real exercise.

Exercise

For one day only, commit to listen to yourself. What are the words rolling through your head? Get a notebook and as you hear them, jot them down. Just for a day.

There are two points to this exercise. The first one is to hear what you have been saying to yourself. Secondly, doing this exercise will allow you to get in the flow of listening by bringing the white noise out of the background.

At the end of the day review your notes. What are the common denominators? List them below.

1. _____

2. _____

3. _____

4. _____

5. _____

As you look over this list what do you see? Do you make derogatory comments to yourself? How often? How many of the comments are positive?

As I have run this exercise in workshops over the years it's always fun to hear from participants about their experiences. Most are stunned at the sheer amount of negativity that is directed at ourselves. One participant made the comment, "If I had a friend talk to me like I talk to myself, I would not tolerate it." She's right. Most of us would not put up with that friend.

Awareness in how we speak to ourselves is the first step (but a huge step) in changing our effectiveness in business. The next step is finding the limiting beliefs and then changing them.

Ready?

Five Things to Remember From this Chapter

1. Our beliefs are powerful and dictate our behavior.

2. Beliefs are a creation of experiences and self-talk.

3. Once that belief is established we continue to believe it until we are presented with evidence to the contrary and even then our brain fights the change.

4. Self-talk is a natural part of being human. The key is changing its tone from negative to positive.

5. To change our behavior, we must root out our limiting beliefs and change the self-talk.

Chapter 4
Breaking Up Is Hard To Do

Steve is a very interesting man with a diverse history and strong religious beliefs. He joined one of my productivity programs because he was experiencing low sales figures. Despite the fact that Steve had all the skills plus a large SOI, his business was not supporting his family. That was a big problem for him… not just financially but emotionally.

One of our exercises was uncovering limiting beliefs. Very quickly an interesting belief revealed itself around Steve. The problem was he had guilt over money. You see he grew up in a family whose life centered around the church. This particular church is one that promotes service, healthy living, family, equality, and dedication to the community above wealth and possessions. The first twenty years of his life was spent in an area where there was no financial class system; everyone was the same.

His business had been created in the spirit of service, which fit his belief system. But as it grew and he began making more and more money his belief system was conflicted. The result was every time his business increased he stopped doing the activities needed to increase the business. Steve's limiting belief was that you cannot serve your community and profit from that service.

Steve's limiting belief may seem extreme but actually I've seen it many times in salespreneurs. This belief was hidden deep inside. His income was the physical manifestation of what he believed. The clues were in his activities.

Do You Have Limiting Beliefs?

We begin the search for your limiting beliefs with an assessment to see what clues are present in your activities. Just as a reminder… no one here but you and paper, so be honest!

Circle the answer that most closely applies.

1. I intend to call contacts each day, but somehow the time goes away before I'm able to call.

5 – Not true
4 – Mostly untrue
3 – Neither true nor false
2 – Mostly true
1 – Always true

2. When I think about talking to someone about my services, I feel nervous.

5 – Not true
4 – Mostly untrue
3 – Neither true nor false
2 – Mostly true
1 – Always true

3. When I explain my business to someone, I negatively anticipate what they think about my business.

5 – Not true
4 – Mostly untrue
3 – Neither true nor false
2 – Mostly true
1 – Always true

4. I think I am good talking on my feet about my business and choose not to have a written and rehearsed script.

5 – Not true
4 – Mostly untrue
3 – Neither true nor false
2 – Mostly true
1 – Always true

5. I feel promoting my services to my SOI is a bad idea.

5 – Not true
4 – Mostly untrue
3 – Neither true nor false
2 – Mostly true
1 – Always true

6. I am concerned that my SOI will think less of me if I promote my services.

5 – Not true
4 – Mostly untrue
3 – Neither true nor false
2 – Mostly true
1 – Always true

7. I spend less than two hours a day performing active (that means talking to people) prospecting.

5 – Not true
4 – Mostly untrue
3 – Neither true nor false
2 – Mostly true
1 – Always true

8. My SOI does not know that referrals are important to my business.

5 – Not true
4 – Mostly untrue
3 – Neither true nor false
2 – Mostly true
1 – Always true

9. I prefer to prospect "cold" leads that do not know me.

5 – Not true
4 – Mostly untrue
3 – Neither true nor false
2 – Mostly true
1 – Always true

10. I have to spend time preparing myself emotionally for prospecting.

5 – Not true
4 – Mostly untrue
3 – Neither true nor false
2 – Mostly true
1 – Always true

11. When I find myself with an opportunity to promote my services, I hesitate.

5 – Not true
4 – Mostly untrue
3 – Neither true nor false
2 – Mostly true
1 – Always true

Scoring: Add up the point value of the answer you circle. How did you do?

0-22 points: Your wonderful mind is getting in your way. It's telling you stories that just aren't true and those stories are keeping you from success (getting what you want).

22-44 points: Although you are fighting the success battle valiantly, you still struggle meeting your goals. Learning how to manage your mind will take your success higher.

Over 45: You recognize that managing your mind is part of a successful business. If you are not yet effectively getting referrals from your SOI, pay particular attention to the Skill section of this book.

The purpose of this assessment is to bring awareness to you that there are clues in your day-to-day activities regarding your beliefs. The next step is to dig a little deeper.

Looking for Limiting Beliefs

Finding your limiting beliefs can be a little tricky because some are so deeply embedded. But there are hints all around us. For example, look for phrases that you repeat frequently or thoughts that you have over and over. What activities are other salespeople doing successfully that you will not even try? Have you experienced a disappointment with a lesson inside? For example....

I had an incident happen one day that pointed out to me one of my limiting beliefs. It came when I was helping my eighty-five-year-old father put mulch in his yard. After a neighbor drove by and waved, Dad told me they were putting their house on the market the next day. They told him about the move three months earlier over coffee.

"Dad," I exclaimed, "why didn't you tell me?" I could see he was puzzled.

"Why would I tell you?" he asked.

"Because I'm a real estate agent."

"Oh... I forgot, " he answered. That was the truth. He had simply forgotten because I never mentioned it.

Here's the point. I believed that because my father had been told I was in real estate sales that he would naturally tell others about my services. The reality is friends, relatives, and acquaintances don't necessarily see us in our sales role. They see us in the light of how we interact with them... friend, family member, fellow committee member, and so on. They simply aren't going to remember that we need referrals without us reminding them. How we are going to do that without ruining our relationships is coming up. The first step is to understand that you have limiting beliefs and these limiting beliefs prevent good decisions in your business.

Limiting SOI Beliefs

Because we are concentrating on working with your SOI, let me get you started with some of the more common ones I see with sales people in that area.

- All my friends know I'm in sales. I don't need to remind them.

- I've done such a good job with that client, they will naturally refer my services.

- Reminding people that I have a service to sell is too pushy.

- There's another person selling that same service that my SOI prefers.

- I will lose friends.

- My friends and family will be uncomfortable with showing me the inside workings of their business or their personal lives.

- Everybody knows I'm new in this business, so if they aren't using me, they probably would prefer working with someone else.

- I've heard that marketing to my SOI doesn't work.

- I'd rather work with strangers… it's easier.

These are just a few I have heard over the years. Do any of them resonate with you? Do you have others?

What Are Your Limiting Beliefs?

As you go forward in identifying your limiting beliefs I have a couple of thoughts. First, limiting beliefs are by nature sneaky and often difficult to root out. Secondly, although we are going to begin the work with three beliefs you may not have identified that many yet and it's okay. The goal here is to give you a model for examination not total elimination of limiting beliefs.

To start off, find a comfy spot, take a pad and pen and consider the following:

- Review the assessment at the beginning of this chapter. Review those questions that you answered either "Always True" or "Mostly True." For example, on question #11 "When I find myself with an opportunity to promote my services, I hesitate," if that is true for you think about why. What belief do you possess that creates a hesitation to talk about your service? Is it a feeling that your service isn't good enough? Is it a feeling your service is like everyone else's? Do you believe people judge you and your profession?

- Look over my earlier list; does anything resonate?

- Are there any phrases that you repeat frequently or thoughts that you have over and over? For example….

Several years ago I was performing a study where my goal was to find common traits of successful salespeople and common traits of unsuccessful salespeople. The structure of the study was a list of questions that were asked during an interview.

One of my interviewees, Cathy, had chosen to participate in prospecting activities where she talked only to strangers. When I inquired about that decision she very quickly said, "I'm not from this area, so I don't have an SOI." Pushing a little further,

I inquired about her husband's SOI. "Oh," she said, "his culture would not be open to Caucasian women prospecting to them."

I got to know Cathy rather well because she later joined one of my weekly classes and during that time I heard her talk frequently about her husband's family being off limits. Certainly that could be true, but the fact that she repeated it so often made me wonder who she might be trying to convince... me or her?

Now that you've had some time to ponder your limiting beliefs, list your top three.

1. _____

2. _____

3. _____

Now that you have identified three limiting beliefs, we need to take a close look at how it hurts you, what your future will be if you continue to believe it, and how is helps you (yes, helps you). Most of our beliefs rather good or bad, limiting or freeing, give us something. A belief that it's wrong to call an SOI member means you don't have to go through any discomfort and we don't have to increase our sales skills. In short, life will be easier if I don't call my SOI. Remember, it will also be less rich.

Exercise: Take each identified limiting belief and place each in a table below. Answer the questions for each belief.

Belief #1:
Why is this belief true?
How does this belief work for you?
Do you know anyone that believes the opposite? How does that work for them?
What happens if you continue believing this?
What happens if you change this belief?

Belief #2:

Why is this belief true?

How does this belief work for you?

Do you know anyone that believes the opposite? How does that work for them?

What happens if you continue believing this?

What happens if you change this belief?

Belief #3:
Why is this belief true?
How does this belief work for you?
Do you know anyone that believes the opposite? How does that work for them?
What happens if you continue believing this?
What happens if you change this belief?

What did you learn from this exercise? Is there a belief that you want to change?

Write them down below:

_____

_____

_____

Did you just handle and eliminate all your limiting beliefs through this exercise? Of course not. Limiting beliefs that have taken a lifetime to build will not be identified or eliminated easily or quickly. But I've seen great progress come when salespeople become aware and willing to name their own limiting beliefs.

Finding Other Limiting Beliefs

My greatest insights have come from writing down my thoughts. For example, many years ago I attended a week long photography workshop in Maine. In addition to learning all the photographic things, we were schooled on creativity. I learned one of the secrets to releasing my creativity was to place all the junk that rattles in my mind on a piece of paper each morning, before my mind became focused on the day's events. I don't edit or call my thoughts wrong. I just write them down. This tool has been one of the most influential changes I made in my life because my limiting beliefs show up on those pages and then I can change them.

I will not pretend for a minute that I do this every day. But when I experience negative emotions (frustration, anger, pissiness) I fall back into the ritual of writing every morning for a few days and I get amazing results.

I can just hear you saying, how am I going to fit an extra fifteen to thirty minutes in the morning to write my thoughts… really? I had the same reaction. But when I looked at where I spent my time, I realized I spent fifteen minutes in the morning standing in my closet just looking at my clothes and wondering what to wear. After that epiphany, I began noticing the time wasters in my day. As a friend of mine says, this is not about time management, it's about priority management. I find time for anything I decide is a priority. You will, too.

Back to Steve

I have to admit that Steve's limiting belief was a challenge because it was so fundamental to his core value system but we attacked it none the less using techniques I will teach you soon.

Interestingly I was in his sales office recently and happened to pass by the sales board. I have to admit, my eyes welled up a little when I saw him at the top.

Five Things to Remember From this Chapter

1. Limiting beliefs are not obvious, but they do leave clues.

2. Not engaging in important activities is one of those clues.

3. Identifying limiting beliefs takes work and introspection.

4. Each limiting belief should be examined to determine if it works for you or should you consider changing.

5. A continued habit to consider is journaling.

Chapter 5

I Want To Go That Way!

Denise was driven. She had graduated from college, completed graduate school and was hired into a job that provided lots of stimulation (and stress). But it was a life she loved. At her workplace she began dating a peer and they soon married. Together they worked hard and played hard until of course, they found themselves expecting. Coinciding with the pregnancy Denise's husband received an amazing work opportunity that meant relocating. They agreed to make the move and she would not work until after the baby arrived.

Denise had the first baby and then the second baby all while remaining out of the workforce. She and her husband made it work financially. Although they paid their bills comfortably there was not enough for the extras… like a nice vacation. One day she was introduced to some vitamins that appeared to be helpful for children. Concerned about all the colds her family contracted, she decided to try them. The results were amazing and Denise soon became a distributor.

Denise believed that selling this product was perfect because it allowed her flexibility in her schedule, allowed her to promote a product she loved, and provide some extra money for her family. These were great motivators but… when Denise was in the company of other mothers, particularly those that remained in the workforce, she could not bring herself to talk about the products.

When Denise began exploring her self-talk she made an interesting discovery… she was embarrassed about her choices. Yes, she was happy to have remained home to raise her children and yes, she completely believed in the vitamins but when in the presence of working mothers she somehow felt inferior to them. Denise was certain that those women were saying "Look at Denise. She was so full of potential and now here she is rotting away. And she's resorted to selling vitamins!"

With that type of belief self-talk going on I would run and hide anytime I saw one of those women and that's basically what Denise did.

Changing

Changing self-talk is two parts awareness and one part conscious effort. Writing your self-talk down in a previous exercise helped you become aware of it. Once you are aware, then what?

I'm going to show you a process for changing self-talk. Before I show you the steps, I want to note that I have found it helpful to give my self-talk a name. Yes, I think of my self-talk as a different person. I find it easier to be objective about and not internalize the negative parts of my self-talk if I attribute it to another person. My self-talk's name is Velma (It's a total coincidence that Velma is my mother's name!).

When you become aware that you have said something negative to yourself, immediately follow these steps.

1. Recognize the negative self-talk.

2. Challenge your self-talk by saying, "No! What you are saying is not true."

3. Defend yourself by saying, "What's really true is _____." Fill in that blank with one of your greatest traits.

4. After naming that great trait, visualize something that brings you wonderful positive emotions. I have made a list of those moments. They include one of my dogs, Frances, when she was a puppy sleeping around my neck. Or the first time I saw the Grand Canyon. Or my wedding day. You get the drift. The idea is to have at the ready a strong positive visualization and corresponding emotion to counterattack the negative emotions.

For example, one day someone gave me two college basketball tickets (a very big deal in my section of the country). But I had no desire at all watch those two teams. I did recognize it as an opportunity to talk to people in my SOI. So I grabbed my list of people, looked at who had given me referrals lately, wrote a quick script to offer them the tickets and thank them for their help with my business. I was ready to go.

Just as I picked up the phone, my negative self-talk started, "Who are you kidding? Everybody you call is going to see right through this. They will know you are using these tickets as an excuse to call and ask for referrals."

The good news is I heard it immediately and was able to say, "No Velma, you are telling a lie. These people know me, respect me, and look forward to speaking with me."

To really cement the new way of thinking I searched for a positive memory and recalled a young couple that I had helped save thousands of dollars. I specifically remembered with pleasure how excited and grateful they were.

See how this works? **The negative thoughts must be interrupted and replaced with not only a positive statement, but also a positive picture with positive emotions.**

Remember, words—picture—emotions. This process can seem silly but I have seen amazing results with just this one action.

Speaking of putting it into action, I found it helpful to make a list of positive emotions that I can use to support the change in my self-talk and beliefs. We will be completing a list of these in the next chapter.

Using this technique helps you stop the negative self-talk, which boosts your energy. However, making directional changes (I'm here and I want to go there) requires changes in our belief system.

The Process to Change Your Beliefs

In the beginning of my sales career I had a heated argument with one of my company's successful salespeople. The argument was over a prospecting method used in our industry. This experienced agent thought it was ridiculous and not worth the effort, but I had success with it. Having someone (particularly someone new) contradict her belief did nothing to change her viewpoint. I didn't understand her stubbornness because I had hard evidence to the contrary.

This is what psychologists call "belief perseverance." Remember in our section about how the brain works, once a belief is accepted by our Believer then our Regulator fights to keep it true. In order to change a belief it has to be replaced by another stronger belief. In my case with the experienced agent, I was telling her not to believe it anymore, versus giving her evidence. My point is if you want to change a belief, it requires significant effort.

You have determined a set of limiting beliefs in the previous chapter. So far you've just begun to embrace that these beliefs may not be true. But that's not enough for lasting change. To create lasting positive change, the limiting belief has to be replaced with a stronger belief, one that you are going to create.

The process of changing beliefs begins with contrasting the limiting belief with the replacement belief. Below are some of the limiting beliefs from a previous chapter and a possible replacement belief.

Limiting Beliefs	Replacement Belief
When I do a good job for a client, they will naturally refer my services.	Doing a good job is key to getting new customers. But it's my responsibility to ensure past clients know that my business depends on referrals from satisfied customers.
Reminding people that I have a service to sell is too pushy.	I'm not selling anything. I offer a valuable service to people and it's my duty to let them know. Otherwise they may make a critical mistake.
Everybody knows I'm new in this business so people would probably prefer to send their referrals to a more experienced person.	I may be new in the business, but everybody in my SOI knows how dedicated I am to my customers and will gladly send me referrals.
There's another person in my group of friends selling the same thing. I think my SOI would prefer to work with them.	Some people will prefer to work with someone else, but many will prefer to work with me. There is enough business for both of us.
My friends know that I'm in sales. I don't need to remind them.	My friends think of me as their friend, not as a salesperson. So I will need to provide gentle reminders to help them remember.

It's time for you to enter your limiting beliefs and create a replacement belief.

Limiting Beliefs	Replacement Beliefs

This is a great exercise. But to really move the meter from the limiting belief to the replacement belief requires some power.

Provide Power to the Replacement Belief

To provide as much power as possible to the replacement belief, we strengthen it with emotion and strong words. We do that by being selective about how it's written and affirmed so that the subconscious will be willing to accept it.

Your subconscious is like a computer… if you put garbage in then you get garbage out. If we tell it to do something, that's what it's going to do. So being careful about how the replacement beliefs are structured is important. For example, if I said, "I need to lose weight" my brain would hear "I'm fat." It's the "I need to" phrase that the brain interprets as "then it currently is not so." The same principle goes for "want to," "should," "could," "would," "wish," "might," and "try." Our brain sees those words as "currently not" and will try diligently to keep us at the current state.

All that being said, here's the characteristics of powerful replacement beliefs.

- **Powerful replacement beliefs are created in the present tense.** They are spoken as if they are true now… I have vs. I want. When you say "I want" what your brain hears is "I don't." Our brains do exactly what we tell them. So it follows the "I don't" command and makes sure that you don't. However, by saying "I have" your brain says, "Okay, I'll make that happen." An example would be "I don't want my friends to think I'm pushy because I ask for referrals." Your brain just heard, ". . . Make my friends think I'm pushy." An example of a better replacement belief is, "I bring such great value to my friends; they regularly send me referrals." See the difference?

- **Powerful replacement beliefs move toward something versus away from something.** For example, saying, "Everyone thinks I am competent even though I'm new in the business." This statement is in the present however, and it implies a "don't want." A stronger way to word this is, "Being new in the business is great because my clients receive better information and a higher quality of service."

- **Powerful replacement beliefs are created in the first person.** These are highly personal and should contain the words "I" or "my" or "me."

- **Powerful replacement beliefs contain emotion/action words.** In the example, "Being new in the business is great because my clients receive better information and a higher quality of service," could be strengthened by adding words that convey emotion. Like, "Being new in the business is exciting for me and great for my clients because they will receive up-to-date information and sensational service."

After many years working with people, I have come to realize that re-writing beliefs is an on-going process. In other words, you may write a new belief and even use it for some period of time, but you might tweak it later as you learn. So don't worry about being perfect at the following exercise of creating replacement belief self-talk.

Using my earlier example of replacement beliefs, I will create corresponding self-talk.

Replacement Belief	Replacement Belief Self-Talk
Doing a good job is key to getting new customers, but it's my responsibility to ensure past clients know that my business depends on referrals from satisfied customers.	I am great at providing customer service. Part of that outstanding service is helping my previous clients provide my business information to people within their SOI.
I'm not selling anything, I offer a valuable service to people and it's my duty to let them know otherwise they may make a critical mistake.	I have created a strong business that treats all people with honesty and integrity. I have a responsibility to tell my SOI so they can be protected when they need this service.
I may be new in the business but everybody in my SOI knows how dedicated I am to my customers and will gladly send me referrals.	Being new in the business is exciting for me and great for my clients because they will receive up-to-date information and sensational service.
Some people will prefer to work with them but many will prefer to work with me. There is enough business for both of us.	I am very confident that I provide the highest caliber of service and know that this service will attract the people who need me.
My friends think of me as their friend, not as a salesperson. So I will need to provide gentle reminders to help them remember.	I bring tremendous value to my friends by providing them market information and by being a valuable resource.

I've created several of these in order to give you examples. But don't let the volume of words spook you. I often suggest to workshop participants that they start with just one and build from there.

Melinda was a participant that did just that. Re-doing her beliefs appeared to be a really big job and I could tell by chatting with her that she was shutting down to the information. So I suggested she take on just one limiting belief. She selected the belief, "I'm too poor to effectively start this business." This belief was creating some significant obstacles for her. Believing she was poor caused her to act poor. Acting poor made others, including potential customers, see her as unsuccessful and who wants to work with someone who isn't successful at what they do?

She envisioned a world of abundance and wanted to create the belief that the world did in fact provide abundance. The resulting replacement self-talk was, "I am rich. Not only do I have plenty but I also have all the skill and talent to make as much as I envision."

Several months later she reported an interesting evolution. This evolution started with personal changes, like she noticed that paying her bills was not the traumatic experience it once was. Then she started noticing changes in the way she thought about herself. This change led to how people saw her. Pretty soon her business was seen by the public as cool and trendy and she was making a profit.

Seems crazy, doesn't it? But think of it this way. We have all seen the person who is desperate for something. The reaction from others is to shy away. However, when someone appears strong, people are attracted. This happened to Melinda. In the beginning, she was acting desperate and people were repelled. But later when she believed herself to be strong, people were attracted to her.

Now it's your turn to write some new and powerful self-talk. By the way, another name for replacement belief self-talk is the term affirmation.

Below, write the new belief and then write out an affirmation.

Replacement Belief	Replacement Belief Self-Talk aka Affirmation

Here's a checklist to use when reviewing your affirmations.

✓ Is it personal (containing either "I," "me," or "my")?

✓ Is it in the present tense?

✓ Does it contain emotion/action words?

✓ Is it moving toward something, not away?

✓ Make sure it does not contain: should, could, would, might, try, will, want to, hope to, but, wish, or need to.

Lots of Information, Where Do We Go From Here?

I've put plenty out there and you may be reeling about what to do with it all. No worries. The next chapter establishes a thirty-day plan in which to implement all this information and begin moving to what you want.

Five Things to Remember From this Chapter

1.   The key to changing your negative self-talk is recognizing it immediately and then challenging it.

2.   Greater change occurs when we empower our words with pictures and emotions.

3.   Creating positive change requires changing our limiting beliefs with replacement beliefs

4.   Our brains are like computers... they are literal so the words we use to create replacement beliefs are very important.

5.   These replacement beliefs are called affirmations.

Chapter 6

What Would You Do If You Could Not Fail?

Do you like to travel? I do. Let's go on a vacation together! You go home and pack a bag, grab your passport, and get some spending money and then we can meet at the airport… okay?

When we get to the airport we can decide where we are going. Can't decide… okay let's board a plane to… nowhere.

Nowhere? Yes, nowhere.

Why would I board a plane that just goes around in circles? Easy to answer: indecision and it makes you feel like you are at least doing something. Your internal conversation may sound like this… Maybe I'd really like to go to Paris. For years I've dreamed about walking up the streets of the Champs Elyse. BUT I've never been there and I'm uncertain about going to country with a different language and culture. Would I be okay getting around by myself? I've heard about those pickpockets in Europe. Would that be a problem?

Perhaps that's too much of a trip. I'll go to St. Louis instead. I really want to go somewhere more exotic but I think it's just too much for me. I know… I'll get on the plane to nowhere, fly around and when we have to land because we're out of fuel, I'll see if I want to get off there. At least I would feel like I'm traveling . . . .

Yes, this may seem ridiculous, but we do this all the time in our careers. We may secretly know what we want to accomplish but are afraid of saying it because we don't really believe it could happen. Or if we say it and fall short then we have to live with the disappointment or embarrassment of failure. So it's really better not to think about the possibilities.

Are you on a plane to nowhere with your business? Working with so many salespeople and salespreneurs in my business, I know this is a missing link in their success.

I want to begin this journey on how to create a referral business by teaching you the first step in how to manage your mind—creating motivation by being a visionary.

We've all experienced the ups and downs of motivation. Some days we feel like we can conquer the world while other days we can barely do the basics. This all seems very mysterious. But you really can be in the driver's seat of your motivation. To do this, let's start with the 411 on motivation.

Motivation comes in two categories: external and internal. External motivation comes to you in the form of (for lack of a better word) bribery. If you do this, you will get that. It's the proverbial carrot and the stick. Parents tend to be great users of this type of motivation. Remember if you don't cry getting a shot you can have ice cream? Or Santa Claus will not bring you gifts if you don't behave? As adults those games continue to be played. Some companies have sales contests, others threaten firing. If you are an entrepreneur then you likely play these games on yourself. Interestingly, this type of motivation works… for a little while but soon loses its power.

But worse, it could backfire. Sometimes the carrot and the stick create contempt and we do the exact opposite. I experienced this in high school when my mother offered me a trip to Europe in exchange for quitting smoking. My response was to smoke more. Did I want to go to Europe? Absolutely. Did I like smoking that much? Not really. In fact I quit a couple of years later.

So why do we have that reaction?

Well, we are all wired that way. All of us want what psychologists call autonomy, which means we all want to feel like we are in charge of our own behavior. So when someone comes along and attempts to change us, we push back. (That can even happen when we try to change ourselves.) That's the downside of attempting to motivate with the carrot and the stick.

Long-term motivation comes from internal motivators. We may be motivated by the need to accomplish, the need for status, or maybe the need to do something important for others. Motivation may be a combination of all three. The point is these motivators must be massaged, even whipped up into a lather, then put in the right place. The catch is no one can do this for you. And if you knew how to do it, you would have already done so, yes? So the question is how?

The answer to that question lies in another question... what do you want? Do you know? When I ask this question in the classes I teach, I find it frequently baffles people. If they do have a response, it's typically unclear. However, having a clear vision of where are you going in your career is the foundation that your career is built on.

I do run into some people who had a dream but lost it. They've pushed it down so hard and so often, they find it's hard to even remember what it was. How do you know if you have lost your vision? Finding a lost vision and creating a new one is accomplished by asking yourself, and really looking at, this list of questions.

Three questions to ask yourself to regain or create a vision.

> Do you know what you want?
> Will you know it when you get there?
> How will it feel when you get there?

Simple questions. Hard to answer.

I met Vicky in one of my productivity classes. As a single mother and a salesperson she worked really hard. When I asked her what she wanted, she looked at me like I was stupid. After she realized I was serious, she answered "Make money."

That's what most people say. I can tell you that money is rarely the answer. Rather it's what the money will buy you. Is it freedom? Status? Respect? Things?

For me revenge was one of my primary motivators when I started my real estate business. I had a very clear desire to see a particular group of people green with jealousy over my success. My fantasy was to get in my new Lexus convertible with them watching. Then drive off laughing knowing that they would be driving home in their old, tired car. I am not particularly proud of this now, but it provided motivation when I started.

When I started digging deeper with Vicky she had the same revenge thing happening. She needed to prove to her ex-husband that she was in fact a better provider than him AND he was a fool to leave her.

Both Vicky and I described our visions as a fantasy… something we fantasized about all the time. The scene was set up in our minds and easily accessible for daydreaming. But best of all thinking about it gave a lovely warm feeling. Just as an FYI, we both ultimately replaced this vision with one that was a little more productive.

But here's the point. The purpose of this book is for you to become comfortable with talking to your SOI about referrals and to build a system to cultivate those referrals. But you will NEVER, and I mean NEVER, put in the time and work to make that happen if you don't understand exactly why you want this. You have to know your purpose, what you are trying to accomplish. It's that vision that will propel you to complete activities that would not normally feel comfortable.

The knowledge of what you want and why it is important to you has to be detailed, not general. When I say detailed, I mean not necessarily in a profit and loss sort of way, but in an emotional way. What does accomplishing this feel like, taste like, and mean to you?

Why It's Tough to Uncover What You Want

When I have this discussion in my classes and I emphasize what you want has to be detailed, someone usually says again,

"Money" and the whole class laughs. And I say, yes, I know, money.

But as we talked about earlier the answer is rarely money, but rather what we can accomplish with the money. To some people the end result is tangible (i.e. a big house). To some people the end is emotional (i.e. feeling successful).

What I've found is deciding what it is that you really want can be rather difficult. Somewhere along the road of life we stop allowing ourselves to think about what we want for fear of the disappointment if we fall short. So we opt not to think about our desires. If we do have an inkling about what we want, we avoid talking about it. If we actually do what a friend of mine calls "putting your mouth on it" then it becomes real and actionable. So, we think, it's better not to even think that way.

That's what happened with Vicky. Her vision of her life; happily married with children living the upper middle-class American dream had vanished. So she no longer trusted the process of deciding what you want because she knew first-hand how fast it would vanish and the disappointment could be devastating. The result is she didn't establish a vision so she was going nowhere. See the vicious cycle?

It's time to think about what you want.

Warning: this is a process. Typically, it takes going through the questions I provide to you, thinking about your answers, reading the question again, thinking about it some more, and so on. (Once in a while, someone will write down their true heart's desire the first time, but that doesn't happen very often.)

Also, the question "What Do You Want?" is really big. So I will help you establish some parameters around it so that it fits you now. For example, some of you want to only think about the next year or the next month... not your lifetime.

As one of my mentors puts it... this is like standing on a warm beautiful beach and we can see the horizon in the distance. However, seeing what's on the other side of the horizon will mean leaving that nice warm beach, which could be too hard. So for vision purposes it may be better for you to just visualize the horizon... where you can still see the shore. Once you are at the horizon you can see further and will be more willing to leave the beach behind.

That's fine. The wonderful thing about this process is that you can duplicate it when you are ready to look out further.

Tools to Determine What Will Motivate You

Below is a list of questions. These questions are intended to stir up your mind and allow you to think about your business in a different way. I always recommend that you dedicate some quiet time to this process and maintain a dedicated notebook for all the exercises in this book.

When you get done answering these questions, you'll have a much better idea of what you like and what motivates you.

1. What activities do you most enjoy in your business?
2. What activities are you best at?
3. Which activities do you like the least?
4. Why did you originally decide to go into this business?

5. How much time do you want to work each week?

6. Describe your perfect work day. You can answer the following questions or just write it out yourself.

   What time do you get up?

   What are your first activities?

   What would you like to do before starting work?

   When do you start work?

   Do you go to an office outside your home or do you work from home?

   Do you keep regular business hours or are your hours more flexible?

   How do you dress to go to work?

   What are your activities at work?

   Do you see or talk to a lot of people?

   To feel completely satisfied at the end of the day, what would have happened?

7. Let's talk money.

   Pretend that it is one year from today and you have just had a record year in your business. You are thrilled! How much money would you have made in your business for this to be true?

   Let's say that all your bills have been paid and you still had lots of money left. What would you do with all that money? Come on… let your mind go wild! DO NOT think about all the reasons why you can't.

Would you build a house?

Would you invest in stocks?

Would you travel?

Would you donate it?

Would you help a family member?

Would you take a month off?

Would you put it in your retirement account?

Would you have plastic surgery?

Would you go on a shopping spree?

So what would you do if you had the money and nothing to stop you?

8. How do you believe you and your business contribute to your community?

9. If someone asked one of your clients to describe you and your business, what would you want them to say?

10. Why are you valuable to your client?

11. What does your client get from their affiliation with you that they can't get from anyone else?

12. Are there disreputable vendors in your profession? How can they harm a client?

Create Your Vision

Answering the previous questions is meant to stir up in your brain what is important to you. Now you can use this information to create your vision, which is the basis of what will motivate you.

But before we start, here's an example from when I created a vision statement for my real estate business.

My business is created from the intention of helping people with the most important purchase of their lifetimes.. .the place that they live. At the end of each transaction my clients feel like I have protected them and they count me as part of their family. They believe selecting me to be their agent was very important to their success and they tell everyone they know. I believe this as well and welcome the opportunities to tell others about my valuable service. The referral business I have created is profitable and I am able to use those profits to invest in myself and my future.

Although I work hard, I understand that to be my best for my clients and my family, time off is important. I make sure that I have time to relax and travel with my husband and friend.

Notice that I have included what is important to me... being considered part of a client's family, feeling strongly myself about my services, having a referral business, being profitable, having money to invest, and making sure I have time for myself.

Vicky, who sells temporary employment services created this vision.

Because I am skilled at listening to the needs of employers and I care about those needs, I am their valued partner. This is important because they trust me and only consider my company when they have a temporary employment need. This relationship provides many referrals and I am honored to service their associates with the same care I serve them. For these services, I receive good compensation that not only supports my family but gives me the ability to invest in my future.

Now let's work on your "if my world was perfect, what would it look like" vision of your business.

_____

_____

_____

_____

_____

_____

_____

_____

_____

_____

Vision Checklist

1. Is your vision about what you want? I want you to avoid talking about what you don't want. If I had this sentence in my example, "I want people to finally value my service," can you see how that sentence is actually

Pushy

negative and is a "don't want" because I'm implying my service has not been viewed as valuable before.

2. Is your vision going *toward* a goal? Make sure you focus on the outcome and it's not a "going away" goal. In my example, I write, *The referral business I have created is profitable and I am able to use those profits to invest in myself and my future.* That is going toward a goal. An example of a going away goal is, "I have paid off my debt and don't have to worry about that anymore." See the difference? In the second example I bring into the vision what I don't want, while in the first example I concentrate on the outcome.

3. Is your vision in the present tense and assumes you already have it? Don't write, "I will," "I want," or "someday." Write like you have it now. Notice that in my vision example everything is in present tense as though it has already happened. This is very important. If I wrote my vision to say "I want to be profitable" that is saying to my brain that I am not currently profitable.

Is your vision what you really want, not what someone else wants? Very often in my workshops I've seen people create a vision based on what they think other people in their lives want. I completely get that. My husband wanted me to be wildly successful, so he would often say things like "When you get to that production level, then we will...". He wasn't saying that to be mean. In fact, he thought these comments were encouraging. But he influenced my vision and I found myself aiming for things I did not necessarily want.

72

Tips about Visions

For many, writing a vision is difficult. Mostly because we rate ourselves. We tell ourselves it's not very good or it's not right. Let me say that it is good and it is right. How do I know? Because there are no wrong visions and all visions are good.

But remember that written visions are a living document. What I mean is they change regularly. As you start moving closer to your vision, you will be compelled to add to or change it. Or as you think about your vision, you may decide that other things are more important to you. Or you may have an upcoming project and create a short-term vision for this period of time.

Create a Vision Board

A good exercise is to create a physical representation of your vision. This reminds you of what you want, because yes, our lives are busy, full of details, and challenges that can get your attention off the vision. So a vision board reminds you of what you want. Plus it's fun to do.

To create a vision board you will need a piece of poster board, a stack of magazines or catalogs, and glue. Simply flip through the magazines or catalogs and pull out anything that resonates with you... even if you don't know why. Just pull them out.

After you have a stack of pages, begin arranging them on your board. Very often you will eliminate some of the clippings from the magazine because they suddenly don't feel right. That's fine. Glue the images that you like on the board. You can take a magic marker and write or draw on the board also, whatever makes you happy. Remember, this should be fun.

Put this board somewhere that you see frequently. Mine hangs in the bathroom where I can see the images while in the shower! I like having my vision board in the bathroom because in the morning my mind is opening to the day of possibilities and because it's a private place for me.

My vision board has a note from a customer about how much I helped them. It has a brochure from National Geographic's trip around the world adventure. In addition to other images, there is a picture of a screened porch that I would like to add on to my house. I also included a picture of me happy and smiling.

Allowing yourself to dream and give these dreams vividness can truly be a fun and fulfilling project. As you will learn in the coming chapters, the most vivid vision wins.

Five Things to Remember From this Chapter

1.   Identifying your wants is the foundation of building your business.

2.   With a vivid image of your future, you will be inclined to build the skill necessary to work effectively with your SOI.

3.   It is okay to allow yourself to dream and not worry about disappointment. It's the dreaming that helps take you where you want to go.

4.   Your vision is very fluid, particularly in the beginning when you are getting the feel of this. Expect that it may change.

5.   Creating a vision board will help you embrace what you want.

Chapter 7

The 30-Day Plan; Putting It Into Action

I can imagine you saying, "Jo, enough already with understanding how my brain works. Just tell me how to implement it!" I totally get that. Good news… we are here. In this chapter I'm introducing a plan to get you started using what you have learned.

Like any good plan, successful implementation requires a few things. The first three are:

1. A strong commitment from you.

2. A strong commitment from you.

3. And, oh, by the way, a strong commitment from you.

Sound scary? Don't worry. I'll remind you how to muster up some strong motivation.

Mustering Up Motivation

You started this journey because you had a problem. Most likely you have been struggling with moving yourself forward. Many people I work with voice that they start every Monday with a new set of goals and actions, things that will move their business forward, but at the end of the week few have been completed and the ones that have been completed weren't all that important. Sound familiar?

One of the most important issues for a business is getting referrals from their SOI. But engaging in the activities that produce referrals can be very difficult because we have some beliefs that are contradictory to the activity. We discussed this in the last chapter. For example, there might be beliefs like if I ask my SOI for referrals, they will think I'm pushy and will never invite me to any social event again.

But you know at the conscious level that referrals mean a better quality business and yes, they mean success. Bottom line: your business will never be what you want unless you tackle the topics of beliefs and self-talk.

Now that you have reviewed why you are here let's contrast it with what you want. In the last chapter you spent some time with the question, "What do you want?" and you were asked to complete a vision board. Creating a vision board is a luxurious activity. To sit and flip through magazines seeing what resonates with you and then putting it on a board is great. You don't agree? (Right now I can hear you shouting, "Are you kidding! How am I going to do that?")

Okay, I know that this exercise can be hard, but it's worth the time. This is your vision, your flag on the hill, your compass for your business. If you can't complete a full vision board, put up a couple of pictures that represent success to you. Make them strong and make sure you can see them every day.

I coached a salesman, Tim, who had four young boys. His annual commissions were way below what his family needed, which caused him great angst. When I asked him what success looked like he would often say, "to support my family." That's a great sentiment, but way too vague.

One day I decided to really press this issue. I know Tim needed a clear visual for what he was after as the key to mustering up motivation. At the end of our conversation, Tim's answer to what success looks like was "tennis shoes." Yes, tennis shoes. You see his boys were embarrassed by discount store tennis shoes they were wearing to school. Success to Tim was being in the position where his boys could wear name-brand tennis shoes. That may sound silly to you, but it wasn't silly to Tim. So all we had to do to complete his vision board was get a picture of a pair of "Air Jordan's" (popular at the time) and post it with a picture of the boys.

Now it is time for you to stop and put together a visual for your dreams. Make sure to post this in a place that allows you to be reminded. This is an important part of keeping yourself engaged in the process.

Great Traits and Emotions

We have two more exercises to complete so that we can have all the tools to engage in our thirty-day plan.

Exercise 1

One last piece in our quest for motivation is remembering what is great about you. We all spend so much time on our deficiencies, yet we wonder why our self-talk is so bad! So let's spend a little time on what is wonderful.

Below, list your life's accomplishments. There is no wrong or right answer and anything you think is an accomplishment counts.

_____

_____

_____

_____

_____

_____

_____

_____

_____

_____

_____

Up next, list your best traits. (These can be personality traits or physical traits.)

_____

_____

_____

_____

_____

_____

_____

_____

_____

_____

_____

_____

_____

_____

_____

_____

_____

_____

_____

The people who love you, what positive things do they say about you?

_____

_____

_____

_____

_____

Don't get lazy on this exercise. Really push about what's great about you. We will need all of these things when implementing your thirty-day plan

Exercise 2

In a previous chapter we talked about how our most powerful beliefs are those that have emotion associated with them. Changing our beliefs will be much more effective if we associate emotions with the new belief. Here's the great thing about our minds… we can borrow emotions from other memories in our life and apply them to the new belief! Your Believer doesn't know the difference. The only thing it knows is there is a wonderful positive feeling associated with that new belief. And because of that feeling, the new belief will take on power.

So our job is to identify moments in your life that created positive feelings. The type of feelings I'm talking about are those that caused that vibration in your stomach. It could have happened with something majestic like standing on top of a mountain and watching the sunset, or holding your child for the first time. Of course these feelings can come with everyday experiences like a cat lying on your shoulder purring. But what we're looking for is that warm sensation or as some people describe it "good vibration" that you experience when you remember those moments.

Take a moment a jot a few down.

_____

_____

_____

_____

_____

_____

_____

_____

_____

_____

_____

_____

_____

We will be using those in just a few minutes to fuel your new beliefs.

Summary of Self-Talk and Beliefs

We are almost there… I promise. I just need to do a quick recap of self-talk and beliefs.

- Self-talk runs continually in our head, and much of it is negative in nature.
- Much of our self-talk is a product of our belief system.
- Our behavior follows our self-talk.

- Our beliefs have been accumulated by experiences over a lifetime.

- We have formed beliefs that are not true.

- Some beliefs are considered "limiting" because they prevent us from growing.

- Like self-talk, our behavior is based on our beliefs.

- Our minds are wired to keep a belief once we have it.

- **We will only be able to grow by changing our belief system and interrupting our negative self-talk.**

How to Interrupt Negative Self-Talk

We looked at the steps for interrupting self-talk in Chapter 4 but let's recap.

Step 1 – Recognize your self-talk is negative

Step 2 – Respond by saying "No, that's not true."

Step 3 – Say to your self-talk, "What's really true is _____." Fill in the blank with something positive about yourself.

Step 4 – Recall a positive emotion moment in your history.

(Remember, by recalling a positive emotion moment in your history, like those we listed above, that good energy becomes associated with the new belief stated in Step 3.)

Years ago when I was first implementing this thirty-day plan myself, I had an unusual experience. About fifteen days in I caught myself with some negative self-talk and responded by saying "No, that's not true." But when it came to saying something positive, I simply could not think of a thing. It was just one of those days. The only thing that popped into my head was, "I have great skin." Shallow I realize, but it was all I could do in the moment. All day long I used the skin statement as my positive self-talk.

That night as I was removing my makeup I realized that during the day I had been told on five separate occasions how good my skin looked! By saying it I was apparently putting out the energy that my skin was great and people picked it up. I have said this before but here it is again… never underestimate the power of other people to read your energy. That's one reason insuring positive thoughts is important.

How to Build New Beliefs

In a previous chapter, you did substantial work on your limiting beliefs, the new belief you would like, and you created an affirmation for that new belief. Now let's demonstrate how to use these affirmations.

To change a belief, a new affirmation needs to be repeated many times for The Believer to allow the old belief to go and put the new belief in its place. **The old belief has to go because our brains are not capable of holding two opposing beliefs at the same time.** Creating an affirmation that has positive emotion and an associated picture will assist the new belief in taking root. Remember… words, picture, emotion.

For this discussion let's use the affirmation, "I bring great value to my friends by being available as an area expert." In your mind create that scenario.

Here's how I would see it (remember I was in the real estate industry)… I'm in my office and the phone rings. My phone directory tells me it's a client I helped with her home several years ago, but I now count her as one of my friends. She's planning on having a yard sale and was wondering if I know the city's sign restrictions. Christie is laughing when saying that she immediately thought of me with that question. I give her the information, ask about the yard sale, and ask her to make sure to keep her eyes and ears open for possible referrals for my business. She says "Of course I will… I always tell everyone about you."

Here's the key to this… you need it to be experiential. What does that mean? Instead of seeing yourself as a third person in that scene, you have to actually be in the scene. Here's an example of being in the scene. When was the last time you were in a boat? Can you remember? Close your eyes and think about it. Remember how the air smelled. Remember the wind against your face. Remember the feeling of going over the waves. Recalling those memories is what I mean by experiential.

So in the scene I described above with Christie, I would feel the chair under my bum, recall the smell of the room, how my phone felt against my face, the sound of the friend's voice. Do you understand the difference?

To re-write the belief in our brain, our brain needs to feel the experience. To our brain *there is no difference* between something it has imagined and something that actually happened. If I truly imagine the physical sensation of a snake crawling up my leg (and I don't like snakes, by the way), my body has the exact same emotional response as if it really did crawl up my leg. BUT this is only true if I actually experience it in my head versus being a third party observer.

I'm sure you have had a similar experience sometime in your life when you saw and felt something vividly and then it appeared. By changing your belief, your mind will make it happen.

The most recent experience I had with this is not sales related, but I'm going to tell you anyway. When I went back to school to get my graduate degree, I basically became a hermit. During the day I held a job with many demands and at night and on weekends I studied. The result was I let my friendships suffer. Most of my close connections were gone—the victims of no attention.

After completing school, I decided to set up an affirmation for redeveloping friendships. I would say the affirmation, follow it with a picture of four women I really liked sitting at my kitchen table drinking wine, and then would apply positive emotions.

One day I had this déjà vu moment when I looked up, and there in my kitchen were those women, drinking wine and laughing. It was exactly like I had pictured it. Obviously I made this happen by inviting those people to my house, but I had not consciously tried to recreate the vision in my mind.

Really, the brain is a powerful thing. So use it well.

Here are the steps to using your affirmation.

Step 1 – Repeat the affirmation.

Step 2 – See yourself in the situation that the affirmation has just created.

Step 3 – Associate a positive emotion.

I found that organizing my affirmations into groups is helpful. To do this, take one affirmation you have created, think through the picture including the vivid imagery, and assign a positive emotion.

Below is the space to create these components. I put an example for you.

Affirmation	Picture	Emotion
I bring great value to my friends by being available as an area expert.	I'm in my office and the phone rings. My phone directory tells me it's Christie, a client I helped with her home several years ago, but I now count her as one of my friends. She's planning on having a yard sale and was wondering if I know the city's sign restrictions. Christie is laughing when saying that she immediately thought of me with that question. I give her the information, ask about the yard sale, and ask her to make sure to keep her eyes and ears open for me possible referrals for my business. She says "Of course I will… I always tell everyone about you."	Years ago my husband and I picked up a new puppy, a Jack Russell, named Frances. On the way home she stared at me and you could tell she was scared. That's when I fell in love with her.

The 30-Day Plan

Now, you're ready to start the thirty-day plan. Here are the activities.

<u>Each Morning</u>

Each morning, complete these activities in any order.

- First thing, jot down some notes in your journal. This does not have to be good, it doesn't even have to be sentences. Just get the thoughts out of your brain and on to paper.

- Complete the three-step process (read your **affirmation**, visualize your **picture**, **feel** your positive emotion) for each affirmation.

<u>During the Day</u>

Your responsibility during the day is to simply stop your negative self-talk using the four-step process we've already outlined. (**Awareness** of your negative self-talk, **say no** to your negative self-talk, substitute **positive self-talk**, feel a positive **emotion**).

<u>At Night</u>

Each night, complete these activities in any order.

- First thing jot down some notes in your journal. Like the morning journaling, this does not have to be well written, it doesn't even have to be in sentences. Just get the thoughts out of your brain and on to paper.

- Complete the three step process (read your affirmation, picture, feel) for each affirmation.

Tips

Over the years, I have found some tips that help me improve the quality and ease of focusing on these activities.

- Start out with one or two affirmations until you begin to feel more confident.

- Start out with something relatively minor so you can see how this works.

- I like to record my affirmations on my phone and listen to them.

- If not recorded on my phone, I have them memorized.

- I typically do my affirmations before getting out of bed.

- Although I am prescribing completing your affirmation two times a day, feel free to do more. Of course the more frequent your affirmations, the quicker the result.

Remember that affirmations are simply directed self-talk. You are talking to yourself all the time anyway, you might as well make sure the talk serves you well. The affirmation process is powerful and can be applied to any area of your life.

Five Things to Remember From this Chapter

1. Motivation for this process requires a good understanding of what you want.

2. To move to your vision, you must learn how to interrupt your negative self-talk and replace it with positive self-talk.

3. You must replace limiting belief with new beliefs.

4. Building a new belief requires creation of an affirmation, an accompanying picture, and an associated positive feeling. You must then repeat it over and over to your mind.

5. Jotting down your thoughts a couple of times per day helps you see where your limiting beliefs are and DE-clutters your brain.

Chapter 8

Beliefs vs. Doubt⋯ And The Winner Is⋯

Justin is a young man struggling in the sales profession. He had been working on a commission only basis for about two years and barely making a living when he approached me about helping him.

On paper, Justin was a perfect salesperson. He was charismatic, he was knowledgeable of his industry, and he had great sales skills. After completing a business analysis and speaking with him, the problem became very clear. It was his belief system.

Justin had established a variety of beliefs that prevented him from fully engaging in sales activities. However he was very committed to the profession for several reasons and was determined to succeed. To help him, I introduced the information regarding beliefs and self-talk, educated him on how to change each, and put him on the thirty-day plan.

He completely embraced the information and faithfully put the concepts into practice. In no time at all, he was reporting significant improvements. Justin even coined the term "my value is open" to indicate that only positive energy was flowing from him. His prospecting activities were up dramatically and his conversion rate was outstanding.

Then, suddenly, nothing. All of his activities stopped and the prospects dried up. When he and I spoke he would only say "my value closed."

I know this sounds crazy. Why would you be receiving everything you want then make the decision to stop it? It may sound crazy, but this is incredibly common. In fact, I expect it. And in this chapter, I'm going to tell you why and then what you can do about it.

Your Regulator

In Chapter 2, I introduced the three parts of your brain. Remember the Thinker who has the responsibility of processing information and making decisions? Then there was the Believer who has the responsibility of storing all our beliefs and helping the Thinker make decisions based on those beliefs. And finally, we have the Regulator. And there's the culprit.

The Regulator's job is to ensure if there are any conflicts going on in the brain these conflicts are resolved. For example, you go to your office on Monday morning and write out your "To-Do" list for the week. On that list is the task to call fifty SOI members and ask them if they know anyone who needs your services. You think that's a great idea and you know that several of your colleagues have experienced success with the same technique. But by the end of the week, you made no progress calling these people (Remember Jack?). You are rather mad at yourself and vow to complete that task next week. Next week comes and goes without any progress. What's going on?

Well, in your brain there's a problem. Your Thinker might have thought it was a great idea, but your Believer thought it was a bad idea. Somewhere in your belief system lives the belief that calling people for the sole purpose of asking for referrals is somehow wrong, inappropriate, or risky. The dispute causes friction between your Thinker and your Believer. This friction causes problems for you. You may find that you are "testy" or emotional and can't really consciously work out the reason. Ever remember this happening to you? Of course, we all have!

So why can't there be conflict between these two—so that your Believer feels like calling prospects is wrong and your Thinker will still carry out the activity? Here's why. **Two conflicting thoughts cannot live in the same brain at the same time.**

Enter your Regulator. Your Regulator is like the referee and gets to decide who is right. How does it decide? Just like a referee looks at the picture of the play, the Regulator's decision is based on who has the strongest vision. If the Thinker has created a strong vision of what will be accomplished by making these calls, then the old belief will be forced out. But if the old belief has a picture that is really strong, the new belief will die. And all of this happens without us even being consciously aware of it.

Whichever belief wins (old or new), that triumphant belief immediately begins talking smack about why the other idea was bad. So in the call fifty SOI members example where the task was not completed that week or the next, the Believer starts heckling the Thinker about that decision. Some of the arguments may be "If you call those people they will not like or respect you anymore" or "I'm sure they already have that product" or "They will not want to do business with someone they know." Sound familiar?

There's another set of powerful excuses our brain sends out. I refer to these as the "consequences." Examples are: being successful means working long hours and never seeing your family. Or I would have to give up _____ for success. Or my friends will feel uncomfortable with me if I earn more.

This system is like the autopilot on an airplane. Most of us are familiar with the concept of autopilot. A button is switched on to keep the plan flying on established co-ordinates. If I decided to fly somewhere else, and tried to turn the wheel the autopilot would pull me back to the co-ordinates originally established. To change the flight direction would require a re-programming of the plane.

That's how our brain works. A destination has been established and the autopilot is turned on. Changing the destination will require establishing the co-ordinances and re-programming them into the autopilot. Affirmations are the re-programming of the autopilot.

However, once the course is changed and autopilot re-programmed, we will experience a period of being disoriented. Nothing will feel quite right and that makes us uncomfortable. It may even make us emotional.

By the way, psychologists call this cognitive dissonance. It is easily identified by a series of excuses made on why not to do something, by a sick feeling in the pit of your stomach, and sometimes by strong emotion. Have you ever said, "I have a bad feeling about this decision?" We think of that as our intuition warning us about something, but really it's our brain attempting to keep everything in order. I will pass on a saying from my mother that she used all through my life. (And yes, let me just go ahead and say she was right.) She said, "Good decisions usually don't feel good."

So when you feel this discomfort, remember it means your affirmations are working. Recognize it… embrace it. That's the feeling of growth and change.

Comfort Zones

Another weapon your brain has in its arsenal is the concept of comfort zones. Most of us know this term but let's understand how it affects progress in the growth of your business.

First, our comfort zone is the collection of our beliefs and the self-image that we have assigned to ourselves as a result of these beliefs. I recently heard someone say, "Oh, I'm just a country boy." That comment let me know how this person saw himself. There's no problem with that at all, until this country boy needs to go to the city to get something he wants. Then he will find himself outside his comfort zone. (When we use these labels to describe ourselves, we think they are benign, but they hold meaning. Sometimes they indicate where we see ourselves in relationship to other people or other things.)

In real estate sales you see this frequently with the price of houses. If the agent sees themselves as servicing first-time homebuyers, they are likely to be uncomfortable when a million-dollar home seller calls. The result could be they will make excuses (without even realizing it) of why they should not take that client. Conversely, the agent that works with million-dollar clients will feel uncomfortable with a $60,000 client.

I taught a class on getting out of your comfort zones when I came up with this bright idea that maybe I should do something uncomfortable. Mind you, I have done many uncomfortable things in my life (like start a business, jump off a thirty-foot pole). But I thought maybe I needed to generate some discomfort for the purpose of personal growth.

I decided to ride a city bus to work. Unlike many metropolitan areas where most people ride the bus to work, in my area I don't know anyone who rides the bus. Despite that, I made up my mind to ride the bus to work the next day. I knew where to catch the bus and I knew it would drop me off in front of my office. I was ready.

But the next morning, I got up late, so I made a slight adjustment in my goal and decided to ride the next day so I would be on time. The next day the weather forecaster predicted temperatures of over 100 degrees… bad day to ride the bus, so I delayed again. The next day I had several errands to run during the day so I didn't ride it then. The next day I had to take a box of books to work, which would have been difficult on the bus. Ultimately, I stopped thinking about it.

Do you see a pattern? To me, these were legitimate reasons. Really, it was my comfort zone trying to keep me in my place. We seek what is familiar to us. Even our friends tend to be people who are in the same culture or socioeconomic class as we are.

And it's likely the amount of business you are doing is a result of "your place."

Plus there's the advantage that it's really nice here. Living in your comfort zone is warm and toasty. There is no stress, you are free from tension. Why leave? Going out there doesn't feel good. There is pain. There is discomfort. But there is also something better. So how do we fight this battle? Your brain may have some powerful tools to keep you in the comfort zone. But I'm going to show you tools you already have to get you out.

Fighting the Battle

Here you are trying to create a new and better future. You've done the work and identified your vision. You've found your limiting beliefs, said "no" to your negative self-talk, and are doing your affirmations twice a day. Yet, as you take several steps forward, you are also taking steps back. The answer to this problem is the picture.

Imagine a rubber band in your hand. Roll it between your fingers. How does it feel? Is it a thick rubber band or a thin one? How long is it? Does it have a smell? Now loop a finger at one end and another finger in the other end and stretch it taunt. Can you feel the tension? Has your face changed reacting to the possibility of it snapping?

One side of this stretched out rubber band represents your current business and the other side represents your vision of a new business. This tension between the sides can't last long or it will snap, so one side has to move toward the other side to release the tension. Which one? It's the one with the most detailed *experiential vision*. Notice that the exercise with the rubber band was described to be experiential. Did you have the image of holding the rubber band and how it felt? That's what I mean by experiential or first-person.

So if you're struggling with the success you're starting to create and find yourself slipping, here's what to do. Go back to the pictures you described that go with your affirmation. How detailed are they? You should be able to describe physical things in the room. You should be able to describe the temperature, the smells, the sounds. Remember, in first person… you are there NOT witnessing it, but experiencing it through your own senses. Couple this with powerful positive emotions and you'll beat the system every time.

Once you have that powerful combination of affirmation plus picture plus emotion, ramp up the number of times you think about it each day. An affirmation usually doesn't last more than thirty to forty-five seconds or so. Although many people will work on a dozen affirmations at any given time, others will work on only a few at a time. I highly recommend that in the beginning you focus your attention on only a few. Once your efficacy increases, you can take on more affirmations.

Over the years I have also noticed that as salespeople get closer to their vision they begin questioning whether or not they really want it. I called it the "consequences" excuse earlier in the chapter. A great technique for helping you avoid falling victim to this is the test-it method. If you have set your vision at a particular goal, go and seek out the person that already has it.

Ask them if you can shadow them for a day. See first-hand what that life looks like.

One of my visions is to live in Paris two months each year. I have the affirmation for this vision and have created an experiential picture - I can feel myself sitting at an outdoor café, I know what I'm wearing, what the wine tastes like. I know the sounds and the smells in the air. But my brain regularly throws up bad consequences of this vision. When I was a child I always got homesick, even on one-night sleepovers. So my belief system tells me, "You'll get homesick, stop dreaming about Paris." To combat this, I used the test-it method. I got a vacation home somewhere close enough to be considered away but still within driving distance of my home in case I had a major bout of homesickness. The result? No problem being away from home. The consequence excuse is gone.

Another weapon we have to fight our comfort zones is mental rehearsal. If I know that there is an uncomfortable situation ahead of me, and I find myself trying to wiggle out of it, then tricking my mind with a mental rehearsal can work. Here's what I mean by mental rehearsal.

Go step by step through the anticipated situation. In my bus example, I could have seen myself at the bus stop chatting with other people. When the bus came, I would ask the driver about the fare, learn how to pay it and then sit in the front row, and so on. Why would I take the time to do this? Because my mind cannot tell the difference between a mental experience and a real one, so I can stretch my boundaries by walking through it in my mind. This technique works best in first person in detail vs. watching it happen.

Just so you know, my decision to get on the bus was fundamentally flawed because I didn't really have a reason other than I'd never ridden a city bus before. So there was no reason to get on the bus. However, if my husband was in the emergency room and I had no other way to get there, then I would have happily gotten on the bus.

One more nasty little trick our mind uses in this battle of change comes after we have accomplished our vision. Say we used the affirmation process and received our reward. Now what? The minute we let down our guard, our brains will attempt to make us go back. The remedy for this is easy... it's setting the next vision. As you near the conclusion of the change you are on, begin considering the next one. Where will you go from here? What is the new vision and affirmations?

With any of these mental fights, ask yourself the question, "Is this my brain fighting change?" The answer is probably yes. Awareness of how our brains work is three-fourths of the battle. Once you understand what's happening... go to war.

Five Things to Remember From this Chapter

1. Our brains cannot maintain two conflicting beliefs.

2. Cognitive dissonance (two conflicting beliefs) may cause a variety of behaviors, including making excuses and being emotional.

3. The Regulator part of our brains is assigned the responsibility of resolving the conflict.

4. The belief that has the most detailed experiential picture will win.

5. Winning the battle is accomplished by awareness, strengthening your vision, increasing the frequency of your affirmations, and mental rehearsals.

Skillset

Chapter 9

May I Have This Dance?

Let's just go ahead and say it. You don't really want to prospect to your SOI. You would really prefer to keep business, business and personal, personal. Great news. You can make that decision. No problem.

One of life's rules is there are consequences to every decision and there are some to this decision. Consequences like less profit, longer hours, and a shorter career. Really? Yes, really.

The benefits of cultivating referrals from your SOI have been acknowledged by experts for many years. The recent change in the economy has created a shift in how consumers think and how they buy. Interestingly, these changes had an effect on SOI as a form of prospecting... it's more essential. Today's consumer has an increased commitment to work with sales professions that they trust. Their tolerance for sales techniques, pushy salespeople, and general bull has gone down. What that means to you is the general pool of cold prospects is shrinking and promoting your services to your SOI is critical.

When starting my sales career I went through my licensing courses, sales training, and was assigned to the same office with a young woman named Nicole. She was remarkable in her prospecting stamina and her conversion skills were great. In other words, she left me in the dust our first year in the business.

Although she performed several types of prospecting she skipped prospecting to her SOI. I was always in awe of her abilities and frankly, her guts. She would find home sellers by hanging out in the local hardware store and would approach people buying "For Sale By Owner" signs. Or she would go to the local baby store and approach pregnant women about their housing needs. These are incredibility difficult forms of prospecting and yet she did them with ease. But what she could not bring herself to do was contact her SOI. Predictably, she left the business. It took less than two years. How did this go-getter of a salesperson (awarded the International Rookie of the Year) flame out so quick? She just wore out.

I realized she was working only with cold leads. That meant she was spending an enormous amount of time finding leads. Of course, because the leads were of lower quality (such as people who wanted to buy but couldn't) she had to generate more leads to make up for the reduction in quality. And because these leads did not know her or trust her, she had a longer conversion process. So on average working cold leads took much longer and more effort than if she was working with warm leads. Did I mention the emotional toll working with only cold leads takes? There's another factor. That's why she burned out.

So knowing this about working with cold leads, let's recap all of the good reasons why you would want to work your SOI.

- No cold prospecting
- Closing rate increases
- Profit per client goes way up
- You work with motivated and loyal clients

- Cost and time of business development goes down
- Long-term success

The 50-30-20 and the 80-20 Rules

There's a rule I refer to as the 50-30-20 rule. Before I explain it, I'd like to ask you about the last time you hired someone.

Think back to the last time you hired a service provider. What I mean by service provider is someone who did something for you, like someone to work on your plumbing or maybe a hair stylist. Why did you pick that person? Think about it… was it a referral or was it an ad? Did you hire them because you believed they were the best for you? Or did you only shop price?

My last service provider was a tree service. I did my due diligence and shopped several. The service I hired was not the cheapest, but two sets of friends used them so they were highly recommended. In other words, I trusted them. And when it came to five large trees that were close to my house, trusting the person bringing them down was important.

If you open the yellow pages and look up plumbers are you going to immediately trust them? No! Perhaps with enough time and contact you will. But if you call a friend who is a contractor and ask for a referral, are you going to trust them right away? Probably so.

That's the way most of us shop. When looking for a product or service, 50 percent of us probably know who we are going to call. If we don't, 30 percent of us are going to call a reliable friend and ask for referral. Only 20 percent of us are going to look to other methods, like surfing the Internet, to find a service provider. That's the 50-30-20 rule.

I have asked hundreds (probably thousands) of people the question, "Why did you pick that service provider?" and the answers are typically an 80/20 split. Eighty percent of the people chose their service provider for reasons that had to do with trust. They liked them, trusted them, believed they were competent, believed they cared about them, and that they were worth the money. The other 20 percent shopped price only. So what do these numbers tell us? People want to buy from someone they like and trust, and will pay more if they believe they are worth it. The key is trust.

To demonstrate this point, let's talk about white ceiling fans. Most of us have purchased a white ceiling fan at one time or another. Shopping for this fan can be difficult just because of the sheer volume available. As you are standing there under all those twirling fans, how do you choose? Most of us shop the price because we have no other way to compare. But if someone knowledgeable were to say, "This fan is quiet and will last for years" then I would happily pay more for that fan versus a less expensive one.

Given you know the 50-30-20 rule and the 80-20 rules, where do you want to be? Do you want to be working with the majority… working within the 80 percent of people who found their service provider on a referral, or with the 20 percent who don't trust you and only shop based on price?

I can tell you based on experience, when you work in the 80 percent you are focusing on building relationships by adding value to the lives of your SOI. When you work in the 20 percent, you are spending your time overcoming objections and trying to convince people to buy your service or product. Hmmm... building valued relationships versus trying to convince people. I know which one I would rather do.

I have given you all these reasons why cultivating your SOI for referrals is important. But I bet you are still not convinced. Right? What's in your way of embracing this as the best-thing-since-sliced-bread is one person. You know the person I'm talking about. That salesperson every one of your peers talks about. Not just talks about but avoids. And we both know this salesperson is avoided because they hound their friends for referrals.

You've been on the receiving end to this pushy salesperson and you simply do not want to be that person. Not even for a successful business.

But you don't have to be. I'm here to tell you that. You see, that pushy salesperson forgot to dance.

What's the Dance?

In my college years there was this guy named David and he loved to dance. The first time I met him was at a party. He and I chatted for a while and before long he asked me to dance. David became my favorite guy to dance with for lots of reasons. First, I liked his style, the clothes he wore, the way he wore them, and he had great taste in cologne. Second, he knew how to dance. Third, he was such a strong leader that I really didn't need to do anything except step into his arms. Fourth and most importantly, when I danced with him, I looked good even though I didn't dance as well as he did. On the dance floor, he and I formed a friendship. We both enjoyed each other's company and we had a mutual respect. Anytime I wanted to go out dancing, I called David.

All the other guys were very jealous of David's ability to swoon the girls. (I was not the only girl who felt this way about him.) Some tried to imitate David. But they didn't talk to a girl before asking her to dance like David did. When a new song started they would run up, grab a girl's hand and attempt to pull her onto the dance floor by saying something like, "Hey baby, wanna dance?" Obviously, the answer was "no." The secret to David was his finesse.

Working your SOI is like a dance. Once they understand what you do and that you are great at it, they'll know they can confidently walk into your arms (or one of their friends can) and you will confidently take the lead. They'll enjoy the fact that working with you looks like a great decision to the outside world (yes, there's always ego). Most importantly, when they need the product or service you provide, they will immediately call you.

And listen to me carefully… you would never, ever walk up to your SOI grab their hand, pull and say "Hey baby… wanna dance?" You like these people and don't want them to feel uncomfortable.

It's about care and confidence and yes, finesse. It's like a dance.

Sphere of Influence System - Overview

I learned after dancing with David for a while, that all of his beautiful dance talent wasn't just raw talent at all. It was hard work and practice. He exercised several times a week and took dancing lessons. Before going dancing, he practiced his dance moves. He took extra care with his appearance. None of his dance talent was by accident. It was by design.

I'm here to teach you how you can have a profitable SOI and great personal relationships, all at the same time. It is completely and totally about the design of your system and your commitment working the system.

What do you mean "system?"

Let me go off on a little side trip for a moment. In the previous paragraph, I used the word "system" twice. One of the things I've noticed over the years is that people react negatively to that word. If I could find another word that described what was needed, I'd use it. So I'm left to define it and hopefully take the angst out of that word for you.

In this context, a system is simply a set of coordinated activities that have been proven to work and are executed on a schedule. And I know that many of the salespreneurs out there are thinking, "I don't want a schedule. That's why I work for myself. I want to be free from all that." Me too.

I know I've said it before, but here I go again. *You will gain incredible freedom and success with structure, meaning you have a schedule to keep.* Yes, that is counterintuitive. But think of it this way. Without a system, you will be in a constant state called "what do I do next." You will be recreating the wheel all the time, leaving your client confused and yourself exhausted.

So let me show you what a profitable "dance" system with your SOI looks like.

Components of an SOI System

A good SOI system design has several components.

1. Organized database including a system for categorizing the names.

2. SOI Expansion system—increasing the number of people that you know is important to the health of your SOI.

3. A communication system. This is a preset schedule of contact with the messages and methods of delivery.

4. A follow-up system. Keeping track of referrals is huge.

5. Thank you system.

All of these systems we are going to talk about in detail coming up. But before we talk about these systems, let's talk about who these people are.

What Does Your SOI Look Like?

Your SOI may be larger than you think. I define an SOI or sphere of influence as anyone who knows you or knows of you in a favorable light. This means anyone who knows you which includes friends, family, people you know through social events, or church, or clubs. It also includes people that you see in your everyday life... the dry cleaner, the bank teller, etc.

Notice in the definition the phrase "knows of you."Who would those people be? Examples would be your spouse's co-worker. You see them at office parties and you hear about them through your spouse, but you don't really know them. You may be thinking "Really? Everybody from my sister to a person I barely know?" Yes, but no worries. I will show you later how to deal with categorizing people.

Now that we have talked about whom your SOI is, let's discuss who they aren't. Many salespeople have identified "farms" that they actively prospect. Farms come in two forms; demographic and geographic. A demographic farm is a group of people that have a common denominator, say they are all single. If you have a product or service that appeals to single people, you may elect to create that farm. A geographic farm is a group of people living in the same area. If your product or service appeals to that group you may create that farm.

What the SOI has that the farms do not is this... a connection to you. The people in the farm don't know you and don't trust you. They are cold prospects. Now is it possible to have someone live in a farm that you know? Absolutely, and they should be on your SOI list so that they receive more personal information. Communication that goes to a farm is more neutral and less productive.

How Many SOI Members Do I Need?

To answer the question of how many SOI you need to build your business, let me tell you a story. Just out of college I went to work for a small software company as a trainer and began dating one of the programmers. This programmer had a roommate that was most certainly a geek right down to his pocket protector. This was before Bill Gates was famous so geeks weren't cute or cool yet. Also the geek was, as we say in the south, unfortunate. Unfortunate is a nice way of saying physically ugly. In addition, he had the worst car I have ever seen.

Because I was dating his roommate, who by the way was cute and hot, we tended to bump into each other at social gatherings. Every time I saw "the geek," he had a beautiful, statuesque girl with him. I found this to be very perplexing. One night it was just my boyfriend and his roommate and I'd had enough gin to ask him how he was able to get these beautiful girls to go out with him. He looked at me over his broken glasses held together by tape (I swear I am not making that up) and said, "Simple, it's mathematics. I ask every woman I meet to go out with me, and let the percentages work. Asking enough women means I can pick the best ones."

So why have I told you this story? Even though we are talking about our SOI, who are the people we like and look forward to serving, this is still a business and there is definitely a mathematical component to be successful. We have to think about and work the numbers. With that in mind, answer these questions.

1. How much money do you make per closed client? _____

2. How much total money do you want to make in this coming twelve months? _____

3. How many clients will you need to *close* to hit your twelve month income goal (divide #2 by #1)? _____

4. On average, how many referrals do you currently receive monthly from your SOI? _____

5. Of the referrals received, how many actually close on average per month? _____

   Note: I know that most of you will not be able to answer this question off the top of your head, but these are great numbers to know. Search it out. Or you can take just one month, calculate the conversion rate, and use it as a sample.

6. What is your referral conversion rate? _____ Divide the answer in #5 by the answer of #4. Move the decimal right two spaces to get the percentage.

   Example:

   I closed on average 1.3 deals from referrals per month

   I received on average 3 referrals per month

   1.3 divided by 3 = 40% conversion rate

7. Using the conversion rate calculated in question 6, how many referrals will you need to receive each month to hit your yearly income goal?

   Calculation: #3 divided by #6

   Example:

   Average money made per client: $3,200.00

   Income goal for the coming twelve months: $50,000

   Number of deals needed to close each month to income goal: 1.3

   Conversion rate: 40%

Referrals needed per month: 3.26 (1.3 divided by .40 = 3.26)

All of this leads us to the big question, "How many people do we need in our SOI to hit the yearly income goals?" The answer is… I have no idea. (Isn't that a disappointing answer!) But I can help you figure it out. There are several variables that will sway this number. Examples are: the quality of your SOI list, the number of times you contact them, the method you use to contact them, and more. I can tell you one thing. The better you are at consistently contacting your SOI in a personal way, the less people you will need on your list. I have a mentor that refers to this as deep versus wide. You can work people deeper, in other words deeper by contacting them more regularly and more personally OR can contact them less frequently and with a less personal message. If you do the latter your will need more people on the list to get the same result.

So where does this leave us? With a good start. We know how many referrals you need each month to meet your goals. Now we have to put a structure into place to begin building your database and communicating with them. As you begin this process, you will become more informed about conversion rates (if you pay attention) and will get the information you need to really work the numbers.

Five Things to Remember From this Chapter

1. Consistently working with your SOI will give your business greater profitability and an easier life.

2. Most people want to work with someone they like and trust.

3. Working with your SOI is like dancing with a gracious partner.

4. Your SOI should include everyone who knows you or knows of you.

5. The number of members needed in your SOI to make your yearly income goals depends on your contact plan. The better you are at consistently contacting your SOI in a personal way, the fewer SOI you'll need to meet your income goals..

Chapter 10

Who Is Your Eleanor?

Frequently I work with groups of salespeople to create production goals and help them build an SOI system to support those goals. It's called the Platinum + program. In that program I was working with a man named Logan. Logan was about twenty-five years old and this position was his first "real" job since college. He had established his income goal for the coming year: $80,000. His plan was to accomplish that goal with a variety of prospecting methods, but his primary method would be working his SOI. He predicted that he would receive three referrals each month and close two of those referrals. All great goals.

One week I asked everyone to bring their physical SOI list. Because Logan had grown up in the area and had the goal of three referrals a month my expectation was a large healthy list of names. Imagine my surprise when there were eight people on the list! Yes, eight. Because I hear lots of things in my coaching practice I have learned how to have a great poker face, but not then. My face contorted in complete amazement.

He saw my shock and said, "What… that's not enough?"

"No," I replied, "that's not enough. You could have moved here yesterday and know more people than that!"

When I asked him more questions, the bottom line was those eight people were the ones he felt comfortable putting on his

SOI list. He knew several hundred people in the area and had considered them all, but had eliminated each one for a variety of reasons. I wish this situation was uncommon… it's not. We all do it. You look at someone's name on your list and start imagining what they are going to say or think about you.

In creating an SOI system, there are several mental hurdles to overcome. This is the first one. We are going to talk specifically about this mental hurdle in coming up. In the meantime, and the reason we are talking about this now, is there has to be volume and quality to this list. Remember we are working the numbers.

So in this chapter, we'll focus on getting that critical start in creating your sphere of influence (SOI). I'll help you define who is and is not in your SOI, we'll look at determining how many SOI contacts you need to reach your goals, how to categorize them into useful lists so you can treat them appropriately, and look at some tips for managing the list.

My experience is salespeople can get paralyzed at this stage. I get that. I've done it. It is the enormity of the project. It's okay… we are going to chunk it down in an attempt to make it easier. You don't know how to talk to your SOI yet about your business and I don't expect that from you. We'll just look at defining and setting up a method for simply hanging on to these critical contacts. So for right now, don't think, just do.

My First SOI List

When I was putting together my SOI list for the first time, I listed everyone's contact information on index cards. Then I went through a laborious process of deciding who I was going to actually put in my SOI. This process was so difficult. Looking at each card I would consider if they would be supportive to my business. Then I would just plain make up stories in my head about why they would not be supportive. Really, my husband considers this period of time one of insanity for me. I literally spent un-tolled hours shuffling those names between the "yes" and "no" piles.

One person in particular sticks out in my mind. Eleanor had been my boss's administrative assistant. Although there was not a direct working relationship between us, we did interact frequently and I really liked and respected her and believed she felt the same way about me. Her index card moved between my two piles most frequently, not because I didn't think she liked me but because she felt far removed. Ultimately, I created a third pile that was called "what the heck." Her name landed in that pile. Surprisingly, she was the first person to call me and give me encouragement in my new profession. I really appreciated that call.

About six months later, I received a call from her. She had switched jobs and was working for the president of a local company. After catching up, she asked me if I would do her a favor... she had been given the responsibility of finding a real estate agent to help them relocate thirty families. Would I be interested in that project? Of course, this call launched my business and set me on an amazing path to success. But I couldn't help but reflect that with one flip of an index card I could have missed that opportunity.

By the way through all of mine and Eleanor's interactions helping these relocating families, I had an opportunity to ask her a question that was nagging at me. She was very aware that I was new in the business when she called me, so why did she risk this big and important project on a new agent? Eleanor looked at me perplexed and responded that there was no risk. She remembered working with me before and she knew my work ethic. I include this story because I want you to wonder who might be the Eleanor in your past?

Step 1: Create a List of Contacts

Get out a pen and paper. Sit somewhere comfortable without distractions and start writing down names of people you know or know of. Don't worry about contact information… just write down the name. There's always a couple of dozen off the top of your head and then nothing. So I've provided a list to help you with this process.

The purpose of this list is to get your mental juices going. I'm positive there are many more "ticklers" that could help you think of more, but this is a good start.

Now you have a list of just names and that's fine. Right now don't worry about who is there or not there. This list will never be complete... ever. It's a living document and will change all the time, so get the idea that there will be a finish line for this list out of your head!

Step 2: Categorize Your SOI

When you look at your list of people, you should see a wide variety. Some you know really well and some you don't know well at all. This disparity between the names is traditionally what trips people up on this whole SOI thing. You can't imagine how you can put together a plan that feels comfortable when communicating with close friends and at the same time, with people you don't know well. The answer is you can't.

Three Categories to Start

The solution is to break your SOI list into categories of people so that you can handle them differently. For example, you may want to have all the people that you consider acquaintances in one category. For simplicity, I recommend three, maybe four, categories at the most. The top three categories I recommend, and will use throughout the rest of this book, are:

1. Acquaintances—these are the people that you know but not that well. If you bump into them at the grocery store, you'll speak, but just briefly.

2. Friends of the Business—these are people who have either done business with you in the past or are people who have indicated that they will happily send you referrals.

3. Fans of the Business—these are people who have demonstrated their belief in you or your product by sending referrals. They are the gold of your business.

Virtually everyone will fit into one of these three categories. There are disadvantages to having just these three categories. For example, the question I get asked most is what about personal friends that do not fit into "Friends of the Business." These are friends who have not done business with you or they have not said they would send referrals. My answer is while they may be friends in your personal life, in your business life I'd put them into the Acquaintances category.

I'm a picture person, so let's look at this graphically.

CATEGORIES – SPHERES OF INFLUENCE

Note from the graphic that the Acquaintance section will probably be your largest category. Next in size will be your Friends category and last will be Fans.

The arrows on the graphic indicate your intention. Your goal for the Acquaintance is to move them closer to the center into the Friends of the Business category. The goal for your Friends is to refer business to you, thereby becoming Fans. The goal for your Fans is to keep the referrals coming. So your contact with each group will be matched to that goal. You may ask if an Acquaintance can go straight to a Fan? Of course, but that's unlikely. If you think about referrals you sent in the past, weren't they businesses you had used or known personally? Probably. I rarely give out referrals unless I feel comfortable about the quality of the service or product. That's why people in your Acquaintance category who become Fans will probably have to become Friends of the Business first.

In addition to syncing your message with the goal of the category, each category group will receive varying levels of contact frequency and personalization. (Exactly what I recommend and how often is coming up in the next chapter.)

Remember, these categories are just suggestions. You could choose to do it very differently. The main warning I offer is don't have too many categories. They will become difficult to manage, which leads to inertia. When I started, I made this mistake. I practically needed a spreadsheet to keep up with my categories and that was just too much. There will always be a person on your list that does not fit perfectly into a category, and it's okay just put them in the best one. The opposite of that is don't have too few categories. One big category is basically a cattle call, and working your SOI requires a bit more individualized attention.

All that being said, I did have a sub-category in my model. I had a group of friends that normally would have been spread over the three categories. The sub-category was there because this group had a common denominator… we all volunteered for the same charity. Why was that important? There were times that I wanted to specialize my contact to them around that charity. For example, one of our sales branches was doing an event where all the proceeds would benefit this charity, so I wanted to contact them about the event. You may want to make similar exceptions, so keep that in mind.

Just as I advised in creating your list, my advice here is not to over think this process. Stick each person in the most practical category for now. You can move them later. If you're not sure what to do, start with the three categories I started with above, Acquaintances, Friends of the Business, and Fans of the Business.

Categories Exercise

While the idea of categories is on your mind, spend a minute working through your categories.

The categories I would like to set up for my SOI are: _____

_____

_____

_____

Step 3: Criteria for an SOI Database that Works for You

Now that you have a list and have assigned categories, it's time to talk how/where to house them. Again, this is one of those places people get stuck when deciding on organization of this list. It may be there are too many different choices, so let's talk about selecting a database. Before we get too far, let me say that just because I say database, doesn't mean you have to use a computer. Lots of people do, but there are effective and very inexpensive ways to do this on paper using file boxes and index cards as well.

Selecting a Database

When selecting a database consider the following functionality.

- Can you create customized categories?

- Can you assign these categories to individual SOI members?

- Can you easily send e-mails to the categories?

- Can you easily print labels for each category?

- How many SOI members do you have or are anticipating having? Can the database handle the volume?

- Can the database handle specialized information (if any) you may need to keep on your SOI?

- Does the database allow you to export the list to other software programs?

- Can you schedule a contact in the future and it remind you? For example, the client's birthday.

One of the things I have noticed over the years has been that salespeople will often over shoot the mark on selecting a database. I was working with a young, tech-savvy salesperson on setting up his SOI. He investigated several different databases and found the one he thought was best, one which also included a monthly payment. Although the one he selected was clearly the best one, it may not have been the best one for him at that time. His company provided a basic database with limited capability to assist new salespeople to get up and going with their business. This basic database was enough to get started but did not have all the shiny bells and whistles of the other one but it was already paid for by his company. So your job is to make a decision if you start with a basic database at little or no expense or invest in a more sophisticated model. It's your choice and your money. If you choose to go with the basic model, ensure that when you are ready to upgrade, you can export your list.

As I mentioned above, I have seen new salespeople start their business using a three-ring binder, or a recipe box with index cards, and do really well. The key is in how and how often it is used. A database provides you convenience and efficiency. It does not provide you motivation or success.

Step 4: Enter Contact Information

I am not going to lie to you. Entering contact information for each of the names on you SOI list is simply a pain. But it has to be done. Fortunately, with today's technology you can practically find out a person's weight! Just schedule a couple of blocks of time, sit down and do this. (Or hire a teenager to do it for you.)

Step 5: Manage Your List

Periodically, your list needs to be reviewed and changes made. These changes are typically moving a member from one category to another. Or the deletion of a member on the list. Regardless, this process should happen on a regular basis. I recommend at a minimum you do this once a year. However, I recommend you don't do it more often than once a quarter.

When you eliminate members, the criteria can be anything you want... they moved, you haven't heard from them, they've experienced something life altering that make them a bad candidate for using your product/service, whatever. Whatever the criteria, try to ensure it falls more on the objective side vs. the emotional side. Remember my example in a previous chapter, when Pam the salesperson called Nancy and misinterpreted Nancy's reaction to the call, and crossed her off the SOI list? One way to prevent this is to only delete from your list at a planned time when you're not rushed, tired, or emotional. If you do your review for deletion on a scheduled interval, rather than on the spur of the moment, that will help prevent emotional culling of people who could help you.

However, there is another database management theory called "buy or die." This means if someone has been added to the list, they have to die to be taken off the list. There are a couple of downsides to this. First, you have the potential of developing a large, unruly list. Second, it costs more because communicating to your SOI list has a price that increases with each member.

Step 6: Expand Your SOI List

Managing your list is easy IF you are expanding your list. And expansion of your list is a critical part of success. It prevents your list from getting stale and increases your probability for referrals. However, expansion is easier to talk about than to do.

When I started organizing my list there were 124 people. With my conversation rate and my income goals I realized quickly this just wasn't enough. My SOI needed to be about four times bigger.

I remember this like it was yesterday. Sitting in my office at work, I wrote down the goal "I will add seven people a week to my SOI list." I almost puked. This seemed so far out of reach, but I had to find a way to do this to reach my income goals. Believe it or not this goal and my husband's car buying experience have something in common.

My husband wanted an Audi for a long time. But being married to a real estate agent meant that the nicest car in the family belonged to me. After I transitioned to coaching and training, the time for a new car came up and we agreed this was his moment to buy his beloved Audi. After we went out shopping he arrived home defeated. Yes, he had found a great car and was considering purchasing it, but on the way home he saw that exact same car several times. He was devastated. He didn't want to buy a common car!

I settled him down by telling him that's just the way our minds work. You see, as he became focused on that particular car, his brain searched for it, and he suddenly saw that car over and over. This is a part of our brain is called the Reticular

Activating System and it is responsible for finding what we have said is important to us. This is why my husband suddenly saw his favorite Audi everywhere.

What does this have to do with you and increasing your SOI? Increasing your SOI has to become important to you. Once it is, you will find opportunities. Simply look for them.

Consider these options for expanding your SOI.

- Join networking groups.
- Join an organization you feel strongly about.
- Do community service work.
- Attend every party you are invited to.

For example, you might have wanted to join a bowling club but thought there wasn't enough time. Well, go ahead and joint because now it's part of your job!

Let me tell you an interesting story. Several years ago, when I first started selling, I met with a salesperson friend of mine. Ashley is very good and very driven, but was at the point of giving up. She had a sales goal she had tried repeatedly to accomplish, but never made it. When we had dinner, she was at the end of the year and once again facing failure. She had decided her goal was not attainable and she was not going to try any longer.

So the next year, she embraced all those activities that had been important to her but she had been avoiding to save time for sales. She joined a tennis club, a walking club, and a cooking club. The next year she not only blew though the goal that had been elusive, she doubled it. The key? She met all of those new people. Not only was she meeting them, but she was engaged in activities that made her happy when she met them!

So… go join something!

Step 7: Have a Plan to Follow Up Immediately

Next is what happens once you meet someone. You have a conversation with them (we will talk about this in detail in an upcoming chapter) and ask for their card. Once you have their card, you go through a series of steps. Below is my model.

1. Write a note or email. The note is simply a "great to meet" you note. Here's an example.

I really enjoyed meeting you today. What a pleasure to chat with someone that has a similar passion and I hope we have a chance to speak again.

In the meantime, if you know of anyone that needs _____, please pass along my card.

With Warmest Regards,

Jo Mangum

Make sure that included in this note are several of your business cards (don't be stingy).

2. Add this name and contact information to your Acquaintance list. I'll describe in the next chapter "dripping" on them to move them up to a Friend or a buyer.

Not everyone feels comfortable with the handwritten note. Some of these preferences will be generational. I can't imagine someone in Gen X or Y (people in their 20s, 30s and early 40s) being as positively affected by a note as a Baby Boomer, but you never know. Think about that person, how they might like to be contacted, and about your style. Your style is an important factor. You don't want to be doing an activity too far out of your style or you will feel disingenuous. That alerts the "BS" meter of the person you have met. In my location and at my age, the written note is considered gracious.

The point of course is to make an immediate contact with the new person.

Prospects

With all this talk about SOI, we still need to talk about where prospects go on your list. This isn't a prospecting book per se, but let me say this. Even though prospects are not considered SOI, they do deserve a spot in your database under the category of "Prospects." In addition, you need a follow-up system established for prospects. Most salespeople fail because they don't follow-up regularly enough and long enough. Use your database to set up a system that "drips" on them, meaning you regularly remind them of yourself and your services.

If the prospect turns out not to be viable currently, I would put them in my Acquaintance category.

The next two chapters cover a lot of the questions you may be having about things, like what is a drip campaign and what to say to people? I want to answer all your questions. So stay with me for the coming chapters.

Five Things to Remember From this Chapter

1. To meet your income goals you must have enough members of your SOI to support the goal.

2. Everyone struggles establishing a list of names.

3. To help with the wide variety name sources, divide your SOI into categories.

4. An SOI list is NEVER finished; it's constantly expanding and contracting.

5. To have a great SOI new names need to be continually added.

Chapter 11
Send, Call, See, Post

Before we talk about the specifics of setting up a contact system for your SOI, let's hit the pause button and once again talk about what we are trying to accomplish.

Working your SOI is unlike direct selling. In direct selling, you are intentionally targeting someone and attempting to close them on your product or service. Working your SOI is about creating awareness and interest in your product/service, so when they have a need or know someone with a need, they will automatically think of you.

To get to that place where a specific SOI member is completely confident in you and looks forward to sharing your contact information takes a thoughtful building of value. And it takes time. Your SOI members can't feel harassed or bothered. They should feel important. Building this respectful relationship is what this chapter is about.

Goal for Each Category

In the last chapter we discussed how there is a goal for each level of your SOI. Let's talk about those goals for each category now.

Acquaintances Goal

Acquaintances are people who know you or know of you in a favorable light. These might be people who know your spouse from work, the people you serve with on a committee at church, or the other mothers at the bus stop. In addition, this category may hold personal friends that have not used your product/service. These personal friends probably have not agreed to be a friend to your business (we will talk about that in a minute). The primary goal for Acquaintances is to move them into the Friends category. They get to be in the Friends category because they have used your business or have agreed to be an advocate for your business.

Friends of the Business Goal

For a person to be in your Friends category they have either supported your business by purchasing from you or they have agreed to send referrals to you. That means you've had a conversation with them where you've asked them to be your eyes and ears out into the community. They understand and agree they will let you know if there is anyone that needs your help. Also, they have been educated on how your business works and that you need referrals to be successful. (I will teach you how to have these discussions, so don't worry.)

Fans of the Business Goal

Fans have demonstrated their belief in me by sending referrals. They understand how your business works and look for every opportunity to help you.

Given these descriptions, Fans are clearly the most important category to you, followed by Friends, then Acquaintances. Your job then is to create a communication system for each category that is appropriate to the category and their importance to you.

Overview - Contacting Your Categories

Let's take each category and discuss how each should potentially be treated.

Contacting Acquaintances

This category typically holds the greatest amount of people and they have not demonstrated that they believe in you. They have made no purchases or no referrals. This being the case, you don't want to spend a great deal of time or money here. But you do want to create awareness and interest in your business as well as keep your name familiar to them. So a regular drip is appropriate. A drip means to remind them of your business and business successes at regular intervals. I will describe several drip campaigns coming up.

Contacting Friends of the Business

Friends should certainly receive the drip campaign given to the Acquaintances. But because this category is more important (they are more likely to use your business and/or refer your business) there should be additional contact planned. The additional contact should be more personal. Examples would be holiday cards, birthday cards, and telephone calls.

Contacting Fans of the Business

Fans should receive everything that Acquaintances receive and Friends receive plus more. The "plus more" means more personal and regular contact.

Types of Communication

There are literally limitless types of communication you can do with your SOI. I am going to describe a few below. The variables used to decide which you use are time and money. Typically salespeople fall into the one of three categories:

- No time, big budget.
- Lots of time, small budget.
- No time, no budget.
- (I suppose there is a fourth category of lots of time and lots of budget, but I have never met one of those salespeople.)

So as you look through these examples, keep in mind what is reasonable for you.

Drip Campaigns

Drip campaigns can be described as regularly spaced communication meant to create awareness and interest in your business.

How

Drip campaigns are traditionally in the form of mail or e-mail. Although a more personal method could be done, like phone calls, the purpose of the drip campaign is to remind large groups of people. The more personal a drip campaign becomes, the more laborious it will be. Although e-mail may be considered the most cost-effective it is generally considered less effective in terms of results. When deciding between the two delivery systems, also consider your audience... who does your SOI most represent? For example, is it the young, tech-savvy group, an over-forty group, or an over-sixty group?

When

Experts tell us that every twenty-one days is the magic number for drip campaigns. Because consistency is a key to success when deciding frequency, consider your time and your budget. If you can only do quarterly contact, that's fine. But do that consistently and well. Don't allow yourself to get overwhelmed. Start at the level that's comfortable. You can always increase your contact. By the way, the best day for someone to receive a contact from you is Tuesday.

What

There are so many possibilities but I will talk about a few. As a reminder "what" goes in front of your SOI should be something that adds value to their lives and should reflect your personality. I am writing this paragraph in mid-March and have received two e-mail postcards this week reminding me that spring has sprung... yes, I knew that and didn't need to be reminded primarily because I live in the southeast and pollen is everywhere. I know these salespeople and that postcard did not reflect either of their personalities and the postcard was not particularly useful to me. Alright, I'm getting off my soapbox. On the lower end of budget would the e-mail newsletter, postcard and on the higher end is the mailed newsletter.

Example - Newsletters

Since newsletters provide more room for content, they are a great option. Traditionally, newsletters will have articles interesting to your SOI, but they don't have to be specific to your industry. Regardless, the newsletter should contain "offers" to the reader that entices them to take action. You might say in your newsletter, "be the first to call me with the correct answer of this trivia question and win…" or "go to my website and register and you will receive a coupon for…" In other words, you will be asking the reader to take some action.

I also found over the years that if the newsletter had a personal note or personal letter accompanying it, my response rate was more significant. Below is a real example of a personal letter I sent.

Dear Friends and Clients,

Hello and welcome to another edition of my newsletter. There's lots of great news and helpful information I want to share with you this month. Here is a quick run-down…

- *Low carb diet… Fact or Fiction*
- *Learn how to eliminate credit card debt*
- *The amazing power of visualization*

One a personal note, I've been on a big home improvement kick. First, I finished my third floor (added about 250 square feet), then we had the house painted, the awnings removed, restitched and cleaned, the windows washed, and installed a new mailbox. It feels GREAT to have all those projects done. We had been putting off painting the house for over a year and our procrastination probably cost us an additional $750 in wood replacement.

My summer vacation was in New York City. I was very lucky and got great tickets to the Madison Square Garden performance of Andrea Bocelli. So much fun! I went with Tom and our friend Marion who goes to New York frequently so we had a great tour guide.

Frances and Ridley have been very busy this summer. There's a large frog living in our garden pond and has provided countless hours of entertainment for them as well as me.

I look forward to hearing from you for any reason, but please let me know if you have friends, family, co-workers, or neighbors who could use a caring, competent real estate professional to help them when buying or selling.

I truly appreciate your friendship and referrals.

Enjoy the issue!

Your Realtor,

Jo Mangum

CRS, GRI, ABR, Broker

The first time I wrote this type of letter, I had an anxiety attack! This felt so personal and so foreign to let a group of people peek inside my life. But people felt a greater bond with me because of receiving this personal information.

Professionally written and mailed newsletters are available to purchase (and you probably should). Producing a newsletter each month is really time consuming. Remember the newsletter can be delivered by mail or e-mail.

Example Postcards

Either by mail or e-mail postcards are a cost effective contact method. However, you have very little space to make any kind of personal connection. The format of the postcard should be the same month-to-month so you don't confuse your reader. Also, make sure you have one point you want to make for that postcard. And always ask for their business.

Several years ago I was assisting a new salesperson to set up her drip campaign. She had all the common obstacles; little budget and little time. Deciding that a newsletter was out of her budget, she started using a business that provided templates for postcards. But she felt they were too "redundant" (her words not, mine). Her conclusion was to produce her own postcard. As an artist she needed something that reflected her business and style. Her decision was to do an 8 ½ by 5 ½ postcard. On one side, she printed her newest work of art. On the other side was a list of gallery openings or exhibits for the month in the town where she lived. This worked really well for her because people looked forward to receiving the artwork (many posted it on the refrigerator) and it reflected her and her business.

Personal Contact Campaigns

For those SOI members that have either done business with you, have agreed to be your advocate, or have sent business to you, personal contact campaigns are important to help you keep your connection to them. A friend of mine, Dan, was teaching a group about SOI and used this example. Dan had always used a particular HVAC vendor. Regardless of the situation, the time or the date, this HVAC vendor was available and reasonable. Dan and his family were renovating a house and using a contractor that he liked and trusted. This contractor suggested that they call his HVAC vendor and Dan agreed without hesitation. He later reflected that the reason he could so easily switch was that he was in the flow with the contractor. So when another HVAC vendor came up, he switched. Your job with the Personal Contact Campaign is to stay in the flow of your Friends and Fans.

How to Stay in the Flow

There is a very wide variety of methods to stay in the flow, but here are the most common.

Personal Remembrances -This would be birthday, anniversary, etc. I know salespeople that track important dates to their SOI and send cards and others that just call.

Holiday Remembrances - Holidays present an opportunity to connect with your SOI. Options include cards, small presents, parties, and other gifts or services. For example, in my business I did the following things.

Christmas: I personally delivered anyone that had used my business in that year and my Fans a poinsettia.

Valentine's Day: This was my annual dessert party that all my Friends and Fans were invited to.

July 4: I delivered watermelons to my Fans.

October: I delivered pumpkins to my Fans.

Regular Contact

To keep my Friends and Fans in my flow required that I also talk to them on a regular basis. My system for the Friends category was to call them each quarter. To do this I had a list of every Friend SOI member on my desk. Part of my daily routine was to call five of these people a day. In the next chapter I will talk about what to say.

For my Fans category I needed to see or speak with them at least once per month. I divided them up into two groups. One group got a call that month and the other got an invitation for coffee. The next month it was the other way around.

Putting It All Together

Although you can put together a SOI campaign in any method you would like, I am going to show you the one I used as a reference.

Activity	Acquaintances	Friends of the Business	Fans of the Business
Monthly Newsletter	X	X	X
Birthday Cards		X	X
Quarterly Calls		X	
Monthly Calls/or See			X
Other Holiday remembrances – Poinsettia, pumpkin			X
Holiday Cards			X
Holiday Party		X	X

Before you panic this was the campaign I used after I was established and making money. The system I would have used, had I known about it in the beginning of my career, is below.

Activity	Acquaintances	Friends	Fans
Monthly Postcard	X	X	X
Quarterly Calls		X	
Monthly Call/See			X
Birthday Call		X	X
Holiday Card		X	X

The budget between these two systems is quite different. In the first example, my annual budget was typically $10,000. That estimate is based on 500 SOI members, which equals $20 per person for the year. In the second example, the annual budget is $2700 for 500 members, which equals $5.40 per person. Of course you could reduce this even more by making the postcard electronic.

Without much of a budget, you will have to use the free methods more frequently and you may have to work a little more (i.e. creating postcards, making calls, etc.). *Do not let your budget be an excuse.* Start slow and build. The only failure here is not doing it.

Social Media

So where does social media fit in this plan? Social media offers several incredible tools that are excellent for creating awareness and interest in your business. Depending on your level of comfort you can create a social media plan that drives referrals. Although there are many great platforms out there (LinkedIn, Facebook, Twitter, Blogging) I am only going to discuss Facebook as an SOI tool simply because it is the most conducive and the most used.

Facebook

A social media site used my many people of all ages. Generally considered a site where you keep friends and family up to date on the happenings in your life. You can enter Facebook and "post" your thoughts as well as upload pictures. Given that your SOI are your friends and family, you will likely be interacting on Facebook with the same people as you are cultivating referrals from. This fact may mean a change in the way you use Facebook.

If you are a current user of Facebook consider what you have been posting and what changes you may need to make. We've all heard of the colossal mistakes people can make with Facebook, but I'd like to share two I recently saw.

One of my friends is a local mortgage consultant and the last time I checked they make money on referrals! This consultant posted a picture of himself beer bonging followed by a detailed description of how drunk he'd become.

Versus a real estate agent that I'm friends with that only posts pictures of houses she has listed or sold. She provides absolutely no personal information.

In between these two examples is the sweet spot.

Be mindful that cultivating your SOI is a 24/7 job. In order for people to use your business they need to trust you and like you. So showing pictures of you drunk erodes trust and only talking about your business does not promote likability.

The general rule of thumb is a 3:1 ratio. For every three posts you make on Facebook, two should be personal and one can be business.

Although I have only discussed Facebook, there are many opportunities to expand and communicate with your sphere via LinkedIn, Twitter, Blogging. If you enjoy social media and find yourself frequently engaged you should create a plan to expand your SOI using these tools. But as a word of caution; nothing is more effective than speaking directly with your SOI. Don't allow yourself to think that communicating through one of these tools is the same.

The SOI Mantra

There is an SOI mantra that I would like to introduce to you. This mantra has been used for many decades (although recently revised to include social media). This mantra can and should guide you in creating your plan. The mantra is: Send, Call, See, Post. Use it wisely.

Exercise - SOI Contact Plan

Let's lay out your first draft of how to contact your SOI member. By the way, you don't have to use my categories or the types of activities I have described. The world is open wide to what you may want to do. Just keep in mind it has to serve your SOI and you have to be able to maintain the system.

Category: Acquaintances

Anticipated number of members: _____

Activity(s):	Frequency	Cost/Annual
_____	_____	_____
_____	_____	_____
_____	_____	_____

Category: Friends of the Business

Anticipated number of members: _____

Activity(s):	Frequency	Cost/Annual
_____	_____	_____
_____	_____	_____
_____	_____	_____

Category: Fans of the Business

Anticipated number of members: _____

Activity(s):	Frequency	Cost/Annual
_____	_____	_____
_____	_____	_____
_____	_____	_____

Total Annual Budget: _____

Total Number of SOI: _____

Cost per SOI Member: _____

No Right or Wrong

There is no right or wrong with this activity as long as you are doing the activity. Many people become paralyzed about the SOI system trying to make it perfect. My first postcard I looked at twenty times and I asked other people to look at it and give feedback. Finally, I worked up the nerve to send it. A few days later I received a call from a friend who told me she really liked the postcard but maybe I ought to consider putting my phone number on it! The point here is just start. You will get better as you do it more.

The Hard Part

I can just hear you saying, "You mean you haven't told me about the hard part yet?"

No, I haven't. The hard part is placing this in your schedule. Where I screwed up when I started was here. I would put on my calendar the big X when the newsletter was supposed to be sent, but I forgot to put on my calendar the activity of getting it ready so that it could be sent. I needed to schedule the "getting ready" activities.

All these activities had to be on my schedule or the newsletter would never go out. So each month, I scheduled a group of tasks that supported my SOI system. This was important because a core principle to having an SOI system is consistency. I promise you will be completely and utterly swamped by the process unless you create an organization system. Here's an example. *Note: I have a friend who was very helpful with the production of this book. When she read the previous section she said to me... "This section is too elementary. You are not stupid and they are not stupid so please delete this part." A few weeks later she called to tell me she had just done it! She was so mad at herself for missing a deadline but it snuck up on her and she wasn't ready. So if you feel like the conversation of how to manage your schedule was elementary... I'm sorry. But you are going to need it!*

Send, Call, See, Post

SUN	MON	TUES	WED	THU	FRI	SAT
		1 Call ?				1
2	3 Prepare B-day Cards for the month. Make coffee appointments for the week.	4 Call 5 people Prepare Newsletter for Printing	5 Call 5 people Send Newsletter to Printer	6 Call 5 people	7 Call ? people	8
9	10 Make coffee appointments for the week. Call 5 people	11 Call 5 people Pick up Pumpkins	12 Call 5 people Deliver Pumpkins	13 Call 5 people Deliver Pumpkins	14 Call 5 people Stuff Newsletter	15
16	17 Make coffee appointments. Call 5 people Mail Newsletter	18 Call 5 people Post	19 Call 5 people	20 Call 5 people Post	21 Call 5 people	22
23	24 Make coffee appointments for the week Call 5 people	25 Call 5 people Post	26 Call 5 people	27 Call 5 people Post	28 Call 5 people	29
30	31 Call 5 people Post					

Measure If It's Working

Another critical piece in creating your SOI system is ensuring that it's working. The very last thing you want to happen is to make this investment and realize a year down the road that the system needs to be tweaked. My suggestion is that for the first two months you keep a record of activities and the business you receive from these activities. Keeping a record is one of the most difficult and gut wrenching things to do. It is also the most incredible thing you can do for yourself. Below is a potential weekly format you could use.

Week of: _____

Activities	Monday	Tuesday	Wednesday	Thursday	Friday	Saturday	Sunday	Totals
Mail/Email								
Calls								
See								
Other								
Totals								
Resulting Leads/ Referrals								

I have to be honest. Keeping a record of your SOI activity takes guts and a genuine desire to succeed. It's just plain hard. But the upside to it is when you see the result, you will be forever changed in a positive way.

I can see now that back in the beginning of my career, I was slack. Yes, I prospected but mostly I bitched that my market was bad and that was why I didn't have the business I wanted. One day my manager asked me point blank if I wanted to succeed.

I said "Of course."

"Then," she said, "meet me in the office Monday morning at 8:30 a.m."

Entering her office that morning, I saw a big flip chart with all the prospecting methods that were common in my profession. She told me that if I wanted to have a long, satisfying career then this flip chart needed to become part of my week. She asked me to record what prospecting activities I had done the previous week. I met with her every week for a year.

On occasion I would walk in and try singing the song, "The market is bad."

But she would flip back the pages and show me that the market was fine. What happened was I had taken a mental vacation about six weeks before.

Later, as a trainer I asked a group of new salespeople to track their activity on paper. The results were interesting. Of the people who tracked (not all of them did), 84 percent hit their sales goals.

I learned not to hide in all the excuses and face up to my activity. And that was the moment I went from selling as a hobby to being a professional salesperson. Think about it.

So let's say you have been tracking your activity and you are not getting the results you want. The likely culprit is two-fold. First, you may be relying on mail/e-mail too often. The second is that you are not making them an offer. Making offers is something we are going to talk about in-depth in the next chapter.

Five Things To Remember From This Chapter

1. Our goal in having an SOI system is to create awareness and interest in our business. This way when they have a need, or someone they know has a need, we will be top of mind.

2. A key to an SOI system is consistency.

3. As a contact moves up from one category to another, increase the personalization of the contact.

4. Create your plan and schedule it in detail.

5. Measure your plan. Measurement of your activity will be instrumental in your success.

Chapter 12

Actions Require Asking

Martha was a new real estate agent. She had recently retired from a job as a school teacher but had always thought she would be great selling houses. Because her retirement plan had been diminished from the recession, she wanted to supplement her income.

From the many years of teaching, Martha had a large SOI and was anxious to begin working with them. She created her SOI list and mailed to them monthly. Despite all of this work, Martha struggled. She called me one day looking for help.

When we started our first coaching session, Martha very quickly proclaimed that she knew she knew how to sell but she was frightened about talking to people. As an example, she told me a story.

Martha and her husband were in a restaurant having dinner one evening when a familiar face approached their table. That face was her son's best friend from high school, John. He had been a regular visitor to her home and she had considered him one of her boys. Unfortunately her son and John had gone to separate colleges so she had not seen him in years.

John had finished college, gotten a great new job back in town and was getting married. Martha immediately realized that all of these wonderful events meant one thing… a house. As they continued talking, Martha's mind began searching frantically for the courage to tell him she was now practicing real estate and ask if he had considered purchasing a house. Soon, however the conversation was over and John had walked away. Martha was furious with herself.

As she described the situation to me I asked her about the feelings she was having in that moment. She said she felt anxious and was worried that telling John about her business would put him in an odd position. She was afraid that he would go from seeing her as a mother figure to a pushy salesperson.

Martha was so consumed with a possible negative perception from John that she never considered having someone he liked and trusted to help him with such a big purchase would be a huge advantage and something he would welcome. It never crossed her mind she could be the best thing that could have happened to him. Hmmm . . . .

Really there are three problems here. First, Martha allowed her negative self-talk to rule her mind. Secondly, she had not convinced herself that she was a valuable asset to clients. Thirdly, she did not have the skills needed for having a good conversation that could end in a potential client.

The skill needed to talk to people and potentially convert them into clients is the topic of this chapter.

The Structure of a Sales Conversation

Did you know that most conversations have a structure? They do. And sales conversations are no different. Maintaining this structure is important to not sounding push... I'll show you why in a minute. First, let's look at the structure.

There are three components to a sales conversation; Rapport, Discovery Questions, and Asking for Action. I call it the RDA model for short. The model below shows the structure of a sales conversation.

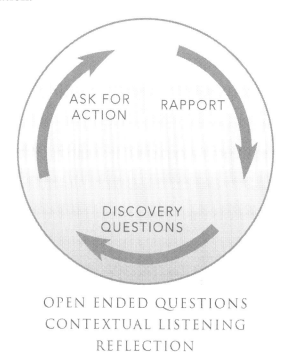

OPEN ENDED QUESTIONS
CONTEXTUAL LISTENING
REFLECTION

Let's look at each part of the three components to a sales conversation, starting with Rapport.

Rapport

The model starts with Rapport. This is where you start the process of building a relationship, which is a key to helping your SOI member feel comfortable. Here's how the process of building rapport starts. When you are speaking with anyone either by phone or in-person, the conversation should always begin with building rapport. There are many ways to do this. I've listed several suggested ways below.

- Pay Sincere Compliments. This is a very strong and quick way to build rapport. Of course, false compliments will be detected, so only use this when you are sincere.

- Be empathetic. Empathy is awareness of the thoughts, feelings, or state of mind of others. In other words, acknowledge it when you see your customer feeling stressed out, tired, or extra happy.

- Discuss common interests.

- Ask follow-up questions. Inquire about their family, profession, and recreational activities. For example, if they mention they have a son who has a baseball game, make a point to ask about the game.

Building rapport has a natural ending. Don't push it, let it evolve. And don't move to the next stage until this one is finished. It's finished when the conversation starts dying down or when they move to another topic.

Discovery Questions

Once you've established rapport, you can start with the discovery questions component of the sales conversation. Discovery is accomplished through careful questioning and listening. This way you can evaluate if this person has a current need for your product or services. Discovery Questions are a powerful way to focus the client. These questions also accomplish the following for you.

- Differentiate you from competitors. *They tell, you ask.*
- Build cooperation and trust.
- Obtain useful information.
- Identify problems or concerns.

There's also a structure to effective Discovery Questions. Here are some definitions to help you create and ask effective Discovery Questions. Discovery Questions are always…

- Open ended—they cannot be answered yes or no.
- Start your questions with the words "what," "how," and "when," "who."
- Non-judgmental—no right or wrong answer.
- Respectful.

Ask Discovery Questions to build a relationship. Think about developing questions using the following categories.

- **Interests:** what's important to them; where they spend their time; what they think about; what fascinates or intrigues them?
- **Problems**: what's bothering them; frustrating them; their dislikes, their fears?
- **Values**: what they hold in high regard; where they put their time and money; what are their politics; what and whom do they admire; what they take a stand about.

- **Philosophies**: their attitude to life and business; how they approach challenges; whether they are optimistic or pessimistic.

- **Motivations**: what makes them take action; their level of commitment; whether they move toward or away from things?

Becoming a master at asking questions designed to get to know people is a vital skill for salespeople.

Used properly, this step can help you gather information, qualify sales opportunities and establish rapport, trust, and credibility.

What are some questions you could use when meeting someone for the first time?

_____

_____

_____

_____

_____

When you feel like you understand if someone has a need for your product or service, then you are ready to ask them for an action.

Asking for an Action

Asking for an Action simply means proposing an offer to the potential prospect or SOI member. If they have a need, you would be proposing an appointment with you. If they don't have a current need then you may be proposing an inclusion to your SOI list with the monthly "drip" of valuable information. During this phase you should use close-ended questions because they provide yes or no answers.

What are some "next step" offers you could make to a potential prospect?

_____

_____

_____

_____

_____

_____

This process of carefully building rapport, being curious about someone and asking discovery questions, and concluding with an offer is valuable to the other person feeling engaged with you.

Below is a sample conversation. In this conversation the salesperson, Judy, is making a "keep in touch" call to one of their SOI members, Sam. The purpose of this call is to say hello and keep her services top of mind. Because that is the purpose, the call should be very conversational.

Judy: Hi Sam, it's Judy, how are you? I haven't spoken to you in the last few months, but wanted to call and catch up with you. How is everything with you?

Sam: I'm great.

Judy: How is everything with Pam and the kids?

Sam: They are doing very well. Pam is really involved with her new career and the kids are looking forward to getting out of school.

Judy: Are you planning a summer vacation while the kids are out?

Sam: We are. We have a camping trip planned and we are going to visit parents in New Mexico, which is also fun.

Judy: I love New Mexico! Although I have to admit, I'm not much of a camper. Tell me about Pam's new career.

Sam: She has started teaching again. You know she left teaching when we had kids but now that they are older she has decided to go back. She's really enjoying it but that makes our lives extra busy.

Judy: Well, I'm really happy for her. Sam, how about you. What's going on with your job?

Sam: I'm still very much enjoying it and hope I will continue there for a while. Judy, how is everything going with you?

Judy: Really well. As usual Tom and I are working hard and playing hard. I know you are busy but I just wanted to say hello and remind you that if you know anyone who needs a caring and competent _____, please give them my name and number. Is there any way I can help you?

Sam: No, we are fine. I always tell people about your services.

Judy: That's wonderful. Please continue to keep your eyes and ears open for me. I really appreciate your help. If I don't speak with you prior to your vacations, have a great time and be careful. By the way, what's the best way to get in touch with Pam? I would like to congratulate her on the new job.

Let's review a few things about this call. First, as identified up front, Judy is just calling to say hello and catch up. She asks several questions about Sam and the family. These questions lead Sam to reciprocate and inquire about Judy. Reciprocity naturally happens in most conversations... by simply asking them about their life they will, in turn, ask about yours. Judy's response is pleasant and personal but she also reminds Sam that she needs his help in her business. In addition Judy has found that Pam is in a new job. Judy needs to re-connect with Pam directly because she is now in the position to meet other people and share information about Judy with them. All in all a perfectly nice keeping-in-touch call. Sam feels valued and cared for, Judy has reconnected, and has the possibility of increasing her SOI through Pam's new job.

Listening

Notice that most of the RDA model is about you asking questions and then you listening. A big surprise for most salespeople is that building your SOI means actually talking very little. We spend the majority of our time and energy asking questions and listening to the answers. That's the process necessary to solving someone's problem, which is the basis of sales.

You would think listening is just the matter of paying attention to what people are saying, but listening is a little more complicated than that because people don't tell you everything. There's an old saying that people are like icebergs; you can only see the very tip. The majority of the iceberg is under the waterline. Your job, therefore, is to listen but also search for other clues about what they want and what they are trying to say. The term for this skill is "contextual listening."

Contextual Listening was an important skill in my past sales profession of real estate. As we performed a needs analysis for a potential buyer or seller, they would often hold back. One day a couple met with me to discuss buying a house. As I asked the regular questions regarding wants and needs in a house, they mentioned several times that they didn't have a neighborhood preference. But I noticed the wife was carrying a Fendi purse, wearing Dolce and Gabbana sunglasses, and wearing shoes that obviously cost a fortune. She was very brand conscious, which meant to me she would be brand conscious in her choice of neighborhoods.

Everyone provides clues to who they are and what they value. Your job is to listen and observe. Here are some tips to increasing your contextual listening skills.

1. **Set your own agenda aside.**

   • Quiet your mind.

   • Put aside judgment.

   • Focus on the client, **not** on what you are selling.

     - What does the client need most?
     - What is important to this client?
     - What are their appearance and language telling you?
     - What is their lifestyle like?
     - How are they motivated?
     - Who is the leader of a couple?
     - How do they make decisions?
     - How do they give and receive feedback?
     - What are potential barriers to progress?

   • Avoid thinking about what you will say next while listening.

2. **Listen contextually for what is really being said.**

   Listen to what is said, what is not said, and what is behind the words.

3. **Listen for:**

   Personal context: What are the beliefs, attitudes, values, and feelings that dictate how the client approaches a situation?

   Situational context: What are the set of circumstances surrounding the client's situation?

As You Listen - Trial Close

As you have a conversation with someone, in addition to listening and asking questions, you must also frequently check for understanding and consensus. In salesperson speak this is called a trial close.

Trial closing is important because you are making sure that everyone is on the same page. Why is this important? Because when you ask for an action and the other person has a question from back at the beginning of the conversation, then you will receive a definitive "no" regarding your offer. Of course, if they didn't express their question or concern, you had no way of knowing they had one.

The solution is to simply insert comments or questions into the conversation that allow for others to express any of their concerns or questions. Here are some examples of the kind of things you can say along the way. "Does this make sense?" "Do you see how that would be important?" "Let me make sure I've understood, you said...." Taking a reading of the other person in this manner before you get to the Ask for an Action stage is just a matter of getting into the habit of asking short questions along the way. Does this make sense?

Asking for Action a.k.a. Closing

I was recently speaking with a salesperson, Chris, who exclaimed that he had lots of prospects, but nobody was buying. So I asked him if he was regularly contacting them by phone or face-to-face (because those are the ways to get the greatest conversion rate vs. e-mail). He responded with yes. Then I asked him what he was saying. Chris replied that he always said that he was just checking in to see if they needed anything and he was available when they did. Bingo... there it was; a classic mistake. He didn't offer them an action.

What do I mean? Every conversation should have this RDA structure applied. After building rapport, Chris should be asking evaluating questions about where they are in the process. Based on these answers, he should suggest an action. It doesn't necessarily need to be a big action. (Like purchasing, for example, because they may not be ready.) But the request for an action should do something to further the relationship, build trust, or help them feel more comfortable with Chris' product or service.

Typically when you ask for an action this question is close-ended, meaning the listener can only answer "yes" or "no." For example, Chris sells life insurance and has been working with a young couple for some time. All indications are that they are struggling with the idea of taking on a monthly payment. Chris has a video that discusses this type of concern, so his close may be to make that video available. His closing question may be, "I have a really good DVD that may provide you with some useful information. Can I drop it by your house this evening?" Notice this is a yes or no question.

A well-done closing is almost organic, meaning that it's a natural progression of the conversation. You have been curious about them as demonstrated in the Discovery Questioning phase and now you propose appropriate action.

The RDA model is a comfortable way to move a conversation forward while understanding the needs of your SOI and providing a solution to those needs.

Breaking the structure of the RDA model is the foundation for sounding pushy.

How to Sound Like a Pushy Salesperson

So what happens in a sales conversation to make the salesperson sound pushy? The answer lies in the RDA model. Sounding pushy happens when the salesperson does very little to build rapport, skips completely over discovery questions, and then goes straight to asking for action. They show no interest or curiosity about the other person. The result is pushy.

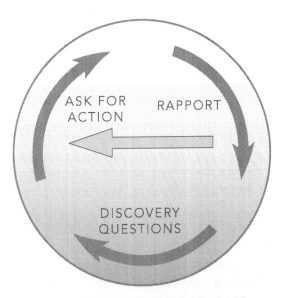

OPEN ENDED QUESTIONS
CONTEXTUAL LISTENING
REFLECTION

Actions Require Asking

Using the above example, Judy would have sounded pushy if she had gone directly for the close. Let me show you how that would look below.

Judy: Hi Sam, how are you doing?

Sam: Fine.

Judy: It's Judy and I was doing my usual call to remind you of my business and hope that you will refer people to me.

Sam: Thanks Judy... sure will!

Judy: Thanks. Talk with you soon.

Certainly pleasant enough and straight to the point but did nothing to continue building that relationship. If your goal is to create a business that is heavily referred, then investing the time in being genuinely interested in someone and listening to them is critically important. Remember, people want to do business with people they believe care.

Objections

Despite your best efforts to ask rich questions, listen contextually and actively, and check for understanding along the way, you will likely run into an objection. First, don't panic. An objection is not a personal rejection. An objection is simply a person saying, "I don't understand and I need more information." Given that definition, an objection is something that should be welcomed, because it provides you the opportunity to clarify.

171

When you get an objection, you can use a model to deal with it that has been used for ages called, "feel, felt, found." This is how it goes.

Feel, Felt, Found

Agree with the prospect's right to have that view—validate their concerns.

1. Let them understand other people have felt that way also.

2. Provide evidence that presents a different viewpoint.

3. Pose a closing question.

Example:

The objection—the prospect believes that you are too new and inexperienced to sufficiently help them.

"Mr. Prospect, I completely understand how you feel and when other clients have heard that I am relatively new they initially felt the same way. But being new has many advantages to you as well. I am enthusiastic, have lots of time to devote, and am up-to-date on the latest advancements in my field. What this means to you is a high level of service, knowledge, and attention to detail. Isn't that the type of service you are looking for and frankly deserve?"

Several years ago I was working with a young salesperson, Ron, who had decided to take on one of the hardest prospecting methods; business to business cold calling. Tough stuff. Using this objection model he would make a call to someone and hear the reasons they didn't want to work with him. After each call he wrote down their objection(s) and wrote a script for how he would react the next time he got that objection. Soon he began getting a lot of business. After hearing the news of his success, I called him to get the skinny.

Ron told me that when he started getting the objections, he wrote down each one and then prepared a rebuttal using Feel, Felt, Found. After the initial five or six objections, he began hearing the same ones over and over so he knew he had the core group. But, he said that it wasn't long before he stopped getting any objections because he had built in the information to his presentation. Brilliant.

I'm betting that, like Ron, you get the same objections repeatedly. Do you know how you will answer?

While we are on the subject of being asked something repeatedly, how often are you asked what you do for a living?

The Elevator Speech

You know it's coming. You will be standing there at a party, a cocktail in your hand and someone will ask the inevitable question, "So, what do you do?" Many of us, in fact most of us say something like "I sell... " What a buzz kill answer! Certainly we don't intend to have that effect on people but we don't really know what to say.

Your answer should do only two things; create awareness and create interest. That's all. Your answer is not expected to make someone swoon with excitement over the prospect of working with you. The purpose is awareness and interest.

The elevator speech is actually a formula. Who + Problem + Situation + Solution.

Who—who is your audience… specifically. Is it a group of people who are geographically linked? Or do they have another common factor in their lives? Examples would be: baby boomers, people with high school children, businesses that sell services, etc.

Problem—what problem do they have? For example, they are dissatisfied with their work life.

Situation—what condition has given this problem some urgency?

Solution—what do you do that solves this problem?

Here's the elevator speech for my business. "My business focuses on salespeople who struggle asking for referrals because they are afraid of being viewed as pushy by their friends. I show them how to go from being viewed as a pest to being considered a guardian."

My husband, who operates a real estate school, could use this speech when he's asked what he does. "My school focuses on people who are dissatisfied with their work life and are now looking for an opportunity to flourish. I help them start a new business by becoming a real estate professional."

Are you starting to get the rhythm? Let's work on yours by jotting down some notes.

Actions Require Asking

Who: _____

_____

_____

_____

_____

Problem: _____

_____

_____

_____

_____

Situation:

_____

_____

_____

_____

_____

Solution:

_____

_____

_____

_____

_____

Put it together:

_____

_____

_____

_____

Remember, we are after awareness and interest. The person you are speaking with should walk away thinking, "Wow, I really enjoyed talking to them."

Likely your first pass at this is not going to produce the perfect elevator speech because this speech is a process and one that is typically pondered. Regardless of the stage that you are in, remember that it must sound and feel natural, otherwise you will not use it.

So how do we get to the point of feeling natural? We use scripts.

Scripts

I know, I know the word "script" makes most people sick to their stomach. There isn't anyone among us that has not experienced the call that interrupts dinner only to talk to a person who mispronounces your name, then proceeds to read from a very stilted script about a product you don't want or need. But before you skip ahead in the book, just hear me out.

Virtually every accomplished professional in the world follows a script. My brother is an airline captain. Not only does he have a welcome script for the passengers, but he also has a script for the flight crew, a script that he follows when speaking with the tower, and a script for practically every possible situation that could occur. He has these because he wants to instill confidence in his passengers and crew. And he has scripts so he does not have to think about everything he says or does... it just comes naturally. Does he have some amazing talent to articulate? No! He has practiced his scripts a lot. That's what professionals do.

Maslow, the psychologist that brought us the Hierarchy of Needs, is also responsible for bringing us stages of learning. These stages can be applied to scripts.

Stage 1—Unconsciously incompetent. This stage is identified by a belief that scripts are not appropriate or needed. The person at this stage believes that they will be better off "shooting from the hip." (My experience is they shoot themselves in the foot.)

Stage 2—Consciously incompetent. This is the first interaction with the script. Boy, it sounds awful. But if they will just hold and practice they will go to the next stage quickly.

Stage 3—Consciously competent. Okay, so the script is really sounding good, although it takes thought when saying it. But with just a little more effort, the next and final stage is just around the corner.

Stage 4—Unconsciously competent. This stage is where the script has become assimilated. You don't even have to think about it.

Yes, getting to stage four is a lot of work. So is losing countless potential prospects because you don't inspire confidence with your words. My recommendation is that you take just half an hour each day to rehearse scripts. Make sure to say them out loud. (They sound different that way.)

Two of the most successful salespeople I know are two women who are friends. Years ago they both decided to increase their sales skills and to hold one another accountable to the process. The plan they devised was to call each other each morning on their daily commute to practice scripts. Each morning they called and rehearsed scripts all the way to work. Amazing commitment with amazing results. Both are consistently named a top salesperson in their company.

Five Things to Remember From this Chapter

1. Speaking with your SOI requires a specific set of skills.

2. The RDA model is the structure of a conversation. Violate the structure and you will sound pushy.

3. Knowing how to ask Discovery Questions, perform Contextual Listening, Trial Closing, and Overcoming Objections are the skill sets all salespeople need to communicate well.

4. An Elevator Speech is mandatory.

5. The only way to sound strong and inspire confidence is to practice your words repeatedly.

Chapter 13

The Belay

I often joke to workshop participants that I have literally made every mistake there is in sales, which isn't far from the truth. But thankfully, I learned a lesson from each and every one. One of my whoppers was luring myself into the belief that all I needed was a strong relationship with my SOI to get the business I wanted. My ideal was people who know and like me would supply me with an endless amount of referrals without me having to ask.

That was ridiculous. The fact I discovered is to build, expand, and maintain a good SOI, and therefore have endless referrals, requires the education of clients on what you want and expect from them.

Painless Training

Right now I can almost hear a collective gulp! But nobody said that talking to your clients had to be painful for you or for them. In the previous chapter I introduced the structure of a sales conversation called the RDA model. In this chapter I'm going to show you how to train your SOI without awkwardness or being "pushy." (I'll bet your getting tired of that word by now. But bear with me.) We are going to look in detail at conversations under the following scenarios.

- Meeting a new person who you want to add to your SOI.

- Running into an old acquaintance that you want to add to your SOI.

- Asking for referrals from a prospect.

- Asking for referrals from an SOI member.

- Asking an SOI member to become a referral team member.

As we go through each of these categories, I'll show you representative scripts. Remember that these scripts are guidelines for you to start with. You can and probably will create your own customized scripts. To be a true professional, practice your scripts until they sound like you.

Meeting a New Person

Meeting new people is very important to building a strong referral business. People may come and go from your SOI, so you should have a regular supply of newcomers. I recently heard a speaker give this visual of what an SOI looks like. You are driving your car to where you want to go. Along the way you are meeting people and asking them to get in your car and go for a ride until you have a lot of people in the backseat. On occasion when you stop at a light one or two will jump out of the backseat. Therefore you have to be continually asking people to get in to fill those vacancies.

Meeting people and having a conversation that makes them excited about getting in your car is the part that most salespeople hate. Getting them in your car is easy if you have one thing… value. Let's look at an example.

Marion is a mortgage lender and is focusing on building her SOI. She has been invited to a housewarming party of a client she has just recently assisted. She finds herself standing beside someone she doesn't know.

Scenario 1 - Marion and Jeff (Jeff has no current need for Marion's services.)

Marion: *Hi, how are you. My name is Marion.*

Jeff: *Hi Marion, I'm Jeff.*

Marion: *Jeff, how do you know our hostess?*

Jeff: *We are neighbors.*

Marion: *Are you from this area?*

Jeff: *Actually I'm not. I'm from the Pacific Northwest.*

Marion: *What brought you here?*

Jeff: *I transferred with a company. So far I really like it here.*

Marion: *Which company brought you here?*

Jeff: *I came with the Research Institute.*

Marion: *What do you do with them?*

Jeff: *I work with drug studies.*

Marion: *So are you new to the neighborhood?*

Jeff: *Yes, I recently bought a house here and really like it.*

Marion: *That's wonderful. Do you remember who your mortgage company was? I'm in that business.*

Jeff: *Honestly, I don't.*

Marion: *As a service to my past clients and friends I have a blog that keeps you up on what's happening in the lending business. This is important to you because as a new homeowner the mortgage industry will impact you selling or perhaps refinancing. What I do is send you a link monthly. What this means to you is being educated and being in the position to make good financial decisions. Does that sound interesting?*

Jeff: *Actually, it really does. We all know how important the mortgage industry is to the economy so I would like to keep up.*

Marion: *Great, I just need your preferred email address. Jeff, do you have a business card with you? Here is mine.*

Jeff: *Here's my best address and here's my card. I look forward to receiving that.*

Marion: *It's really been great talking with you. Here's my card. If you know anyone that needs a caring and competent mortgage lender, please pass along my information.*

Jeff: *I'd be happy to.*

As a replay, Marion did a great job with the RDA model. She built rapport up front then moved the conversation forward by asking questions meant to understand more about Jeff. When Marion discovered Jeff did not have an immediate need for her services, she made him an offer to join her SOI by receiving her blog, offering him something of value. Now she has the ability to drip on Jeff and potentially turn him from an Acquaintance to a Friend of the Business OR a Fan of the Business. Also, let's look again at the offer Marion made to him. I've emphasized three areas that are particularly important.

Marion: *As a service to my past clients and friends I have a blog that keeps you up on what's happening in the lending business.* **This is important to you because** *as a new homeowner the mortgage industry will impact you selling or perhaps refinancing. What I do is send you a link monthly.* **What this means to you is** *being educated and being in the position to make good financial decisions.* **Does that sound interesting?**

Marion used two terms, "This is important to you because" and "What this means to you is." Those two phrases outline for her listener why they want to join her list. It makes it easy for your listener to understand the benefit. Make sure to use similar language when talking with anyone.

Secondly, Marion provided a trial close at the end, when she said, "Does that sound interesting?" to give Jeff an opportunity to voice any questions or concerns. This is important. Your listener needs to feel involved and intrigued by your offer.

As a follow-up to the conversation, Marion could send Jeff a note expressing how much she enjoyed meeting him and enclose some additional business cards for potential referrals. Jeff should then be added to her drip campaign.

Let's look at a similar scenario with the same two people, only this time change Jeff's situation.

Scenario 2 - Marion and Jeff (Jeff may need a mortgage.)

In this scenario, Marion and Jeff meet under the same circumstances, but Jeff does have a need for Marion's mortgage services.

Marion: *Hi, how are you. My name is Marion.*

Jeff: *Hi Marion, I'm Jeff.*

Marion: *Jeff, how do you know our hostess?*

Jeff: *We work for the same company.*

Marion: *That's great. How long have you worked there?*

Jeff: *I have worked there for about five years, but just recently came to this area with them.*

Marion: *How do you like our city?*

Jeff: *I really like it. I came from the Pacific Northwest and even though this area is very different, I'm enjoying the different culture and weather.*

Marion: *Which area do you live in?*

Jeff: *Right now, I'm renting an apartment in the eastern part of the city while I decide where I want to buy.*

Marion: *You know I'm a mortgage lender and helped Julie get a great financing package on this house. I have a free service I offer people who are considering buying called "Your Mortgage Game Plan." We would spend about a half hour talking through your financial goals with a house and give you ideas of how to best structure a mortgage for your situation and life. This is important because selecting the best mortgage is critical to your financial health. Is that something you would be interested in?*

Jeff: *That sounds great, but I'm really not looking for a year so I think it's not quite time.*

Marion: *No problem, I completely understand. In the meantime, why don't I sign you up for my monthly e-newsletter. This will provide you information on what's happening in the industry so when you are ready you will be educated. Does that sound like a good idea?*

Jeff: *I would like that.*

Marion: *Great. Do you have a card? Just write down the best e-mail address to use. And here's my card.*

Jeff: *Great, thanks.*

On the replay, again Marion did a wonderful job building rapport and asking questions. When she realized that Jeff may have a need for her services, she made an offer to meet with him and review mortgage options. When he rejected the offer, she presented another offer that required very little from him but had a benefit, which he happily accepted.

Marion's next steps would be to use his card to write him a note about their meeting, add him to her e-newsletter list, and make a reminder in her calendar to call him in about six months. Why six months rather than a year? Marion will want to make sure she is ahead of him beginning the buying process. Also, after six months of seeing her e-newsletter he is more likely to be open to accepting her offer for an appointment.

Running into an Old Acquaintance

When running into an old acquaintance your business goal is to reconnect and add them to your SOI. To accomplish this you simply follow the RDA model, which is actually easier under these circumstances with an old acquaintance than the previous situations where you don't know them. After building rapport, ask questions in three main categories: family, work, and fun.

In the following scenario, Rich is a financial planner and has just run into Mike, an old college friend.

Rich: *Mike! How are you... so great to see you.*

Mike: *Rich, long time. How have you been doing?*

Rich: *I'm really great. How is Pam?*

Mike: *Well, it's not just Pam anyone. I also have two-year-old twin sons.*

Rich: *Wow... you are a father. How time flies. What are you doing these days?*

Mike: *I work in sales with a pharmaceuticals company.*

Rich: *Do you still water ski for fun?*

Mike: *Not much anymore. Having twins leaves very little time for that. Hopefully when they are older, I will teach them how to ski. Rich, what's going on with you?*

Rich: *Since I last spoke with you I got married. Her name is Heather. No kids yet, but hopefully soon. My business is financial planning. In fact, I focus on people exactly like you...*

young family starting out. This is important because most young families are concerned about a college plan and in building a solid future. I show them how to structure their financial life where they can save and invest without living like paupers. I regularly hold free half day seminars that lay out the basics. What this means to you is it gives you the education to make good decisions about your family's future. Is that something you would be interested in?

Mike: *Absolutely, you hit the nail on the head... it's all a bit overwhelming.*

Rich: *Great. Do you have a card? I can send you an invitation. But in the meantime, I would really like to have coffee and talk about old times. Could you do coffee on Friday morning?*

Mike: *That's a great idea. Friday is perfect.*

Rich did a great job of executing the RDA and asking the questions involving family, work, and fun. These questions led Mike to naturally ask for information about Rich. If Mike had not done that, Rich would still have asked Mike about coffee. When Rich realized during the conversation that Mike might have a need for his services, he gave his elevator speech and made him an offer of the invitation to a workshop.

So why did Rich ask Mike to coffee even after he agreed to attend the workshop? Mike is Rich's demographic farm (young, married, children, starting a career) with twins. Twins means Mike and his wife probably participate in twin groups, which could potentially expose him to another sphere. Lastly, Mike is in sales, which means he is naturally more open to the ideas and processes behind building a referral business. These things mean Rich might be able to add Mike to his Fans of the Business category. This relationship could bring value to them both.

Asking for Referrals

I see this mistake all the time… a salesperson who believes that if they do a good job, their client will naturally refer people to them. It would be so great if it was true. But it's not. Not even close.

The problem has nothing to do with whether or not the client likes and trusts the salesperson. The problem is the client doesn't understand how it all works. Clients generally believe that business for their friends in sales falls out of the sky into their lap. They don't understand that many of us "eat what we kill."

So your job as a salesperson is to make them aware you need referrals. And, secondly, to ask them to help you find people that may need your services. Yes, I know that's easier said than done.

When to ask, you say? The obvious answer is often and repeatedly. Your drip system should be asking for referrals with every contact. That being said, asking directly for referrals is very powerful and will reap you many rewards. There are many opportunities to ask for referrals including when you first begin working with someone, at the conclusion of your work together, and on regular calls to your SOI.

Asking at the Beginning of Your Working Relationship

Most businesses have an analysis period where the person providing the product or service is learning to understand the client's needs. This is an ideal time to ask for referrals.

Here's a scenario to illustrate how this is done.

Salesperson: *While we are getting to know one another I would like to tell you about how I do business. My business is built on trust, care, and exceptional service. This is important for you to know as my new client. One demonstration of this philosophy is that most of my clients come to me as a referral from other clients. These referrals are important to the health and growth of my business. I make sure to tell this to new clients like you because while we are working together you are talking to friends, co-workers, and family. And may find that some will be interested in my services as well. If you run into that, I would love the opportunity to assist them as well. Is that okay?*

In the script above, you let the client know up front that referrals are important to your business and that those referrals were well earned. In addition, this is a prime time to identify other people who may be interested.

Here's a more direct scenario.

Salesperson: *I have found that many times when I'm working with someone they have a friend or family member that has the same need. Who would you know that could use the same service?*

Note in the second scenario (or script) that I asked "Who would you know...." Versus "Do you know...." I did this because most often when you ask, "Do you know anyone that would use the same service" the immediate answer is "no." However, when you ask "Who would you know that could use the same service," the open-ended nature of the question prompts them to think about it.

I have demonstrated two different ways of asking for referrals because each of you has your own personal style. I want to emphasize that all your communication should reflect your style. The first was more consultative in nature and the second was much more direct. The other factor that affects your approach besides your personal style is the style of the listener. For example, if they are direct, then a more direct style would be appropriate.

Asking At the Conclusion of the Working Relationship

Many businesses have a natural conclusion in the relationship... the deal is done. This is another natural place to verbalize your request for referrals. You can do this by simply saying, *"I have very much enjoyed working with you and would appreciate it if you gave my name to anyone needing a _____. In fact, let me ask you, "Who do you know that may need my services?"*

Because they are in a positive spirit about your business, this is one of the best times to ask directly.

Asking for Referrals During Regular Calls to Your SOI

As we discussed before, regular contact is critical to cultivating referrals from your SOI. Part of that system of contact should include regular phone calls. These calls have a two-fold purpose: to re-connect emotionally and to remind them that you appreciate referrals.

Following the guidelines of the RDA model is important in this situation. As before, you want to use questions about family, work, and fun. Because this is an interactive conversation there is a strong likelihood that you will be asked about yourself and your business. Be prepared to be upbeat (even if you don't feel that way) but still authentic.

What if things aren't going as well as you'd like? If you are in a business that is struggling, don't answer a question about your business as "fantastic." The listener will feel deceived, which leads to loss of trust, which leads to the loss of an SOI member. A possible answer to "how's business" may be some of the following scenarios.

You know, it's better. I am very lucky to have a lot of people who believe in me and give me great referrals. As a matter of fact, who do you know that would benefit from my services?

Depending on your industry segment you may have a need to expand your explanation of the market. The point of this is to reiterate that your business depends on referrals and ask who they may know.

While this is on your mind, take a few minutes and jot down a script for the question, "How's business?"

_____

_____

_____

_____

_____

_____

_____

_____

_____

_____

_____

Asking Your SOI to be a Member of Your Referral Team

Remember how we categorized your SOI? Here's a reminder.

- Acquaintances (people who know and know of you in a favorable light)
- Friends of the Business (people who have used your business or worked with you in another business)
- Fans of the Business (people who regularly refer people to your business)

One of your jobs is to facilitate movement in these categories. For example, you want Acquaintances to work with you and Friends to refer to you (and working with you is okay too). I hear you asking can't Acquaintances refer to you too? Of course! But they are most likely to work with you first. Regardless, here's the rub... you have to ask. Specifically, you have to ask the people in your Friends category for their help.

I have to admit that as a professional salesperson there are several activities required for success that I simply don't like. Most of these activities I can blow off or find my way around with only a little consequence. However, there is one big exception... asking for help.

Why do you need to ask for someone's help? Because if you love referrals, you have to train your SOI to locate people who need your service. So your choices are to work other prospecting methods that take twice as long and produce less profit, OR become comfortable with asking for help. Bummer.

I realized how difficult this was for me many years ago when in an absolute moment of incredible stupidity I agreed to climb a thirty-foot pole and jump off the top. Since I'd never experienced this type of activity before, I was not familiar with the harness-pulley-rope system that is used to keep you safe.

I was introduced to the "belay," which I learned is the person who is assigned to keep your rope tight and you feeling secure. In fact, working with the belay was one of the points of this exercise. As you start climbing your rope becomes slack. This reduces tension in your harness, which makes you feel very vulnerable.

My instructions were that when this happened stop and say, "Belay, I do not feel safe and I need your help. Please tighten my rope."

I quickly learned something about myself... even hanging off a thirty-foot pole with my life in peril, I found asking for help difficult. The words literally choked in my throat and tears welled up in my eyes as I finally eked out the words.

Many people have this same problem. We somehow believe that asking for help is a sign of weakness. Saying that we need assistance is showing someone we are vulnerable. But if you are in the business of getting referrals, asking people for help is extremely important.

Ironically, when I've witnessed others ask for help, they appear strong. I am endeared by the thought that they have asked me. I find them sincere and genuine in their efforts. Because of this sincerity, I really want to help them.

The key is in the way you ask. So how do you ask for help so that people have a positive response and you feel comfortable? Below is a structure that can assist you.

- First and foremost remind yourself what value you will be bringing to a referral. Holding that strongly in your heart will allow you to be more powerful.

- Identify exactly what you want prior to asking. Having clarity allows you to be specific within your message, which leads me to my next point.

- Make it easy for the listener to understand what you are asking by being specific.

- Ensure them that you take referrals very seriously and will live up to their confidence.

- Thank them in advance for them helping you.

- Give them an opportunity to ask for help in return.

Here's a scenario to illustrate.

Steve, I really need your help. Many young families are in the vulnerable position of being underinsured. My goal is to help twenty-five families this year re-assess their insurance needs. So I was wondering, would you be my eyes and ears out in community and let me know if you hear of anyone who may need my assistance? I promise you that I will take great care of anyone you refer. I would really appreciate it. Is there anything I can help you with?

Just as a reminder, the script above should be presented at the end of a conversation with your SOI. It should not be the entire conversation.

The question for you then is, "What would happen in your business if you became 100 percent comfortable with asking for help?"

Find out.

Here's your chance. Think of a member of your SOI and write out how you'd ask them for help.

_____

_____

_____

_____

_____

_____

_____

_____

_____

With this script make sure to say them aloud because the script will sound completely different. Be sure to say your scripts aloud after each revision and make changes and practice your scripts until you feel comfortable.

Five Things to Remember From this Chapter

1.   Maximizing the number of quality referrals you receive from your SOI requires that you speak to your SOI members in a specific way that trains them to help you.

2.   Begin training your prospects from the very beginning about the importance of referrals to your business.

3.   When talking to your SOI always ask about family, then work, and then fun.

4. When presenting an offer, make sure to tell them why this offer is important and what the benefit of the offer is to them. End the offer with a question, or trial close, which will allow them to ask questions.

5. Remember, most people consider someone asking for their help a compliment.

Chapter 14

Pushy – Finding Your Process

Several years ago I was working with a company as their Sales Performance Director. This company had on any given day 800 salespeople. My job was to understand the needs of the sales force and react to those needs with training and coaching programs.

In that job I had heard the "pushy" question a few thousand times and had developed some programs that mirrored much of the information in this book. But never, ever had the idea of a book entered my mind until one event happened.

I had been invited to a live webinar led by a sales guru. Every industry has them; they are the person that is held above all others as the quintessential knower of all things sales. My respect for this person was deep and I had incorporated many of his teachings into my curriculum.

When the guru opened up the microphone for questions a man from New Mexico asked "the" question, "How do I ask for referrals from my friends and family and not sound pushy?" Everyone held their breath waiting for magic words that would solve this problem. The guru said, "Great question. Get yourself a good script. Who else has a question?"

Fury literally whelmed up in my throat. I couldn't believe what was just said. There were hundreds of people on this webinar hanging on his every word and the best he could do was "get yourself a good script?" Really?

I am one of those people who does not get mad often and when I do get mad it's short lived. Typically within thirty minutes a temper tantrum is over. Not this time. The disbelief at the shallowness of that answer so outraged me I was talking about it for days.

After hearing about this over and over my husband couldn't take it anymore. "Stop talking about it or do something about it; one or the other," he proclaimed. "What would I do about it?" I asked. His answer was "The best way to make sure the right information gets out there is to write a book."

That's how this book was born. As I am writing this last chapter it has been seven months and three days since the official start of the book. Not only has writing a book been a huge challenge and ironically a practice in applying many of the principles of this book but life has been a challenge. I have lost both my father and my sister during these seven months.

Ensuring that I leave this book on the right note is important. After pondering this thought I have decided to help you by pulling the ideas together; cliff notes if you will. In addition I have presented some practical applications of this information.

Actions - Mindset

The first section of this book focused on creating the business you want by examining and changing your mindset. The main principles of this section are below.

How Your Mind Works:

- There are three sections to your brain.

- The Thinker is the section that is used to evaluate information, makes perceptions, makes associations and makes decisions. The Thinker uses the Believer to inform these functions.

- The Believer is the culmination of our experiences and the resulting beliefs. This history helps the Thinker make decisions. One of the challenges is... sometimes our Believer is wrong.

- The Regulator has the job of keeping the status quo in the brain. But when there is a fight between the Thinker and the Believer, the Regulator is the mediator.

Your Vision:

- Answer the question "If the world was perfect and there were no barriers, what would your business look like?"

- Create an affirmation that transports you into that vision of your business.

- Create a picture board that represents this vision.

Limiting Beliefs:

- Review the limiting beliefs you discovered in the exercises.

- Recognize other limiting beliefs when they pop up.

- Alter these beliefs by creating affirmations that reflect a new reality.

Journaling:

- Get in the habit of jotting down thoughts on paper.
- Periodically review these notes looking for limiting beliefs.

Self-Talk:

- Be on high alert for your abusive self-talk.
- When identified, stop it in its tracks!
- Replace it with something positive about yourself.
- Add a memory of a positive emotion.

Affirmations:

- Affirmation is another word for self-talk. However, affirmations are typically intentional.
- Affirmations are composed based on your vision... what you want and where you are going.
- The purpose of affirmations is to alter your limiting beliefs.
- Affirmations should be repeated several times a day.

Obviously, this is the bare bones of the mindset section of this book. If you have not already, I would go back to the thirty-day plan and begin its implementation. Remember to start slowly and take on more changes as your self-efficacy grows.

Actions - Skillset

Use the following steps to establish your basic SOI program.

Step 1: Create the List—Create a list of people who should be in your SOI. Put anybody you think of in the list.

Step 2: Categorize the List—By categorizing this list by their value to your business, you can best manage contact. The more valuable the contact, the more frequency and personalization of your contacts.

Step 3: Select a Database and Enter the Contacts—Look back at the chapters for detail on evaluating databases.

Step 4: Create a Contact Plan—With each category decide on the action to take and the frequency of these actions. Consult the examples and considerations (like budget).

Step 5: Implement the Plan—Remember that even an imperfect plan executed is better than a great plan not executed. There will be lots of mistakes and many things to learn. Be patient... just take action.

Best Practices

Over the years, I have seen many great salespeople in action. Most have developed habits that fostered success. Below are some of these practices that you may find helpful.

Calling Your SOI

I've said it before but it bears repeating; nothing strikes fear in the hearts of salespeople like making a sales call. But there's really nothing more essential to the sales profession. Especially now.

My friend, Linda, has been in the financial planning business for the past eight years. Her first five years saw success and a growth trend in her business. Then the recession hit and she struggled terribly. Last year she approached me about helping her. Reviewing her business analysis I noted she was doing several varied types of prospecting but all of her communication was via e-mail and mail. She never called anyone nor had she ever made any calls. The vibrant economy hid this flaw in her business. Now faced with depletion of her savings, she still would not accept that calling people was essential. Why?

Simply, Linda had a belief that calling and asking for referrals was below her. Given that the old market was not coming back, she had a decision to make; either have a prosperous business or get out. She made the conscious decision to change her prospecting methods and add calling her SOI to the activities. But where to start?

I have another friend who says, "The words have to taste good" meaning we aren't going to do it unless we believe the words we are speaking. So that's where we started. I created a plan that helped her move toward this activity and that's the plan presented below.

Step 1: Create an affirmation—This affirmation supports the ideal of your SOI welcoming your contact. Linda's affirmation was, "My SOI members view me as a valued part of their wealth team and always welcome the opportunity to speak with me." She repeated this affirmation several times a day and strengthened it by adding vivid pictures and emotions.

Step 2: Religiously Perform a "Before-Call" Questionnaire (BCQ). A BCQ is a system where just prior to making a phone call you spend a moment contemplating the call and its purpose. Linda would answer the following questions for each call prior to making it.

- What's the purpose(s) of my call?
- What questions do I want to ask them?
- What value can I bring to them?
- What offers can I make them?
- Reasons why they would want to refer their friends/ family to me.

Having considered these questions, Linda felt and sounded confident in her role. These feelings translated into a good experience for both her and the client.

Step 3: Summarize and Schedule—After the call, Linda would make notes summarizing what happened on the call and schedule any follow-up activities.

This three-step process established a system to change her beliefs followed by adding value to her SOI member. It was stilted at first but as she grew more confident she began looking forward to the calls.

Your Action: Consciously create a process that addresses your limiting beliefs and helps you feel like a valued business.

Find Your Mantra

As an overachiever I approached the sales profession with the idea that whatever worth doing was worth overdoing. This manifested itself by me doing every possible form of prospecting available in my profession. Did that work? Kinda. I met lots of potential prospects but I never followed up with any. What was I thinking? Well, let me tell you.

Every time I picked up the phone to call a prospect, my internal voice, Velma, started chattering. Her words something like… "They will not remember you and you are just going to embarrass yourself. Really, they want nothing that you have." I wasn't even aware that this conversation was going on in my head. I believed there just wasn't enough time to follow-up, which was my Regulator keeping me from extending outside my comfort zone. Ultimately, I threw away the lead.

Then one day that internal conversation rose up to my conscious and I heard it. It was astounding that I would talk to myself that way. No wonder I found excuses not to call. That's when I came up with the idea of creating a mantra. The mantra I created was "They need me."

Taking a piece of printer paper, I taped those words to the handle of my phone. All day long those words stared at me. Every time I picked up the phone, I touched those words. Soon, I started believing those words. The results were so interesting. I felt very comfortable calling them because my service was valuable to them. I am certain that they heard the confidence in my voice and reacted more positively.

Your Action: Create a mantra.

Be Prepared for Negative Emotion

Most salespeople regularly experience some form of disappointment or rejection through the course of their professional life. Whether it's a deal following through or their mother buying from a competitor it can throw a salesperson hard enough to get them off their game. Shaking off negative emotion is important to your success. It's going to happen, so be prepared.

In the study I completed looking for common traits in successful salespeople, I noticed a common denominator in the area of negative emotion. They may wallow in the emotion momentarily but used positive self-talk to recover quickly. For example, several would say to themselves, "That's okay. It's just business and I will move past it."

When it happens to you (and it will) the key is to shake it off quickly. Having a prolonged "pity party" will permeate all of your life. Quickly recognize what your self-talk is saying and replace it with positive affirmations.

Pick Who You Associate With

Growing up it was one of my mother's favorite expressions… "If you lie down with dogs, you're going to get fleas." Of course, she was trying to persuade me to pick my friends carefully. That's what I'm trying to get you to do also.

In all sales organizations there are the doers and the talkers. The doers focus and get the job done while the talkers talk about all the reasons why they can't get the job done. They completely fail to notice that there are people actually doing the job.

These negative attitudes are contagious and so are the positive attitudes. Consider who you associate with. Opening up your mind to bigger possibilities requires associations with people who are already there. Seeing the realization of your dream in someone else makes the dream real. Who do you know that meets that criteria?

Your Action: Ask someone who is accomplished to be your mentor.

Stop Making Assumptions About What Others Are Thinking

When I first started the development of an SOI plan my brain went into overdrive thinking about everyone's reaction to my new career. There were great assumptions made about virtually everyone on the list; none were positive. I created elaborate stories about this person or that person and how they would snicker (yes, snicker) when they received my newsletter. In short, I was rejecting myself before anyone else could.

Oh, the pain these stories have caused me. Creating evil stories about what others are thinking is not limited to my neurosis, we all have this tendency.

One day my husband made a statement where it was obvious he had assumed what I was thinking. I was rather irritated and said to him, "Wow, do you have super powers and know what people are thinking? If you do, go read the thoughts of Warren Buffet and make some money!"

So I ask you, "Do you have super powers and know that people are thinking?" Of course you don't... this is just our brains saying those things to prevent us from getting outside our comfort area.

Your Action: Be vigilant about this type of self-talk; it can prevent you from productive activities.

Build Your Efficacy

I love the word efficacy because of its meaning; the capacity for producing results. Building your efficacy is not about the direct actions (like calling your SOI) but rather it's about increasing your ability to take those actions. How do you do this?

I'm sure there are hundreds of possibilities, but I will concentrate on two that I have seen work well.

Method 1: Being a Lifelong Learner—Back to the study I conducted on successful salespeople. One of the common denominators was learning. They all had ferocious appetites for learning. Most were in the middle of a book at the time of the study and many had a motivational CD in their car.

Although they learned new skills from these books and CDs, more importantly was they expanded their mind to the possibilities presented. When you see that it's possible your mental scope gets widened.

Recently I was coaching a person who had been emotionally beaten down through the recession. One of the casualties was her ability to dream about a bigger life. After that session she met someone who was living a life she used to dream about but had pushed away.

When I last saw her, she was once again engaged in her dream. Learning can do that for you too.

Method 2: Acknowledge Your Success—Isn't it sad... we do not take the time to acknowledge our successes. That's because we spend so much time focusing on our perceived failures. But acknowledging and congratulating ourselves for what we have accomplished (even little things) is important to building our efficacy.

I'm going to describe a practice I have... each Sunday evening I dedicate about one hour away from the rest of the family to sit with my vision. My process is this:

- I read my vision and think about it experientially, which means I think about in the first person. For example, if my vision is living in Paris writing books then I place myself at a café drinking café crème. In that thought I can hear the traffic, feel the seat, smell the city.

- I review activities from the previous week and highlight all of the things I did well.

- I acknowledge those actions I could improve and make notes of how I can improve them.

- I establish my most important priorities for the coming week and then block time in my calendar to work on them specifically.

I'm not suggesting you should do this just like mine, I'm just sharing what has worked for me. When starting it really felt decadent to pat myself on the back for good things. Now I count on that time to shore me back up for the coming week. Without this hour each week I honestly feel like a chicken running around with my head cut off.

Whatever process you use is fine… just use one.

Your Action: Find a process for reflecting on your successes.

Closing Thoughts

This book attempts to span two very diverse topics: The practicality of establishing and implementing a system that generates referrals to your business and the life skill of understanding how your mind works and how to change it.

I decided to take on the task of writing a book on these topics mainly because it needed to be said. Most trainers/experts only talk about the skill of getting referrals; not the mental game of referrals and this is a mental game. Setting up an SOI system really is easy because it's a learnable skill but most people don't establish this system because they can't manage their associated thoughts.

So why does this matter? Because the principles in this book will assist you in creating a referral business but there is a deeper reason…

Knowing beyond any doubt that you can make a living with your knowledge and skills is freedom.

To access additional resources…discussion questions, additional worksheets etc., go to 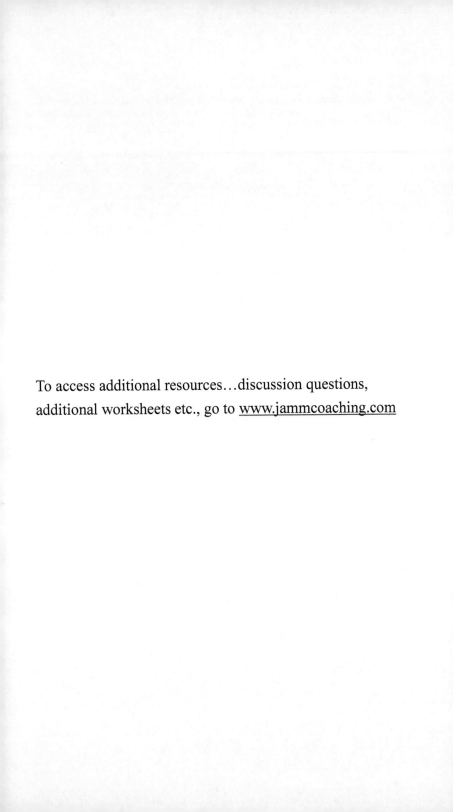www.jammcoaching.com

Pushy

Made in the USA
Lexington, KY
19 January 2014